Not All Magic
is
Black Magick

A Queer Prisoner's Wiccan Anthology

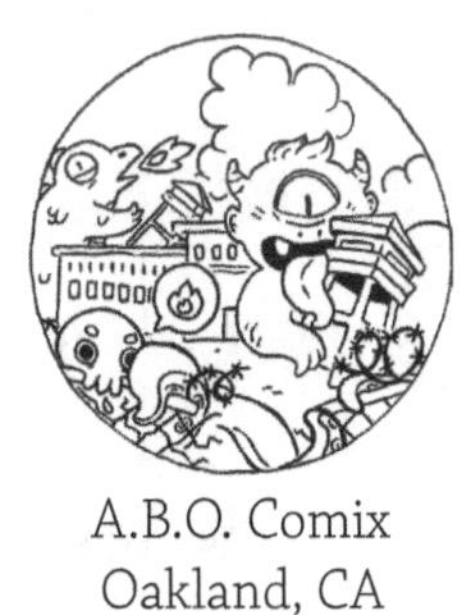

A.B.O. Comix
Oakland, CA

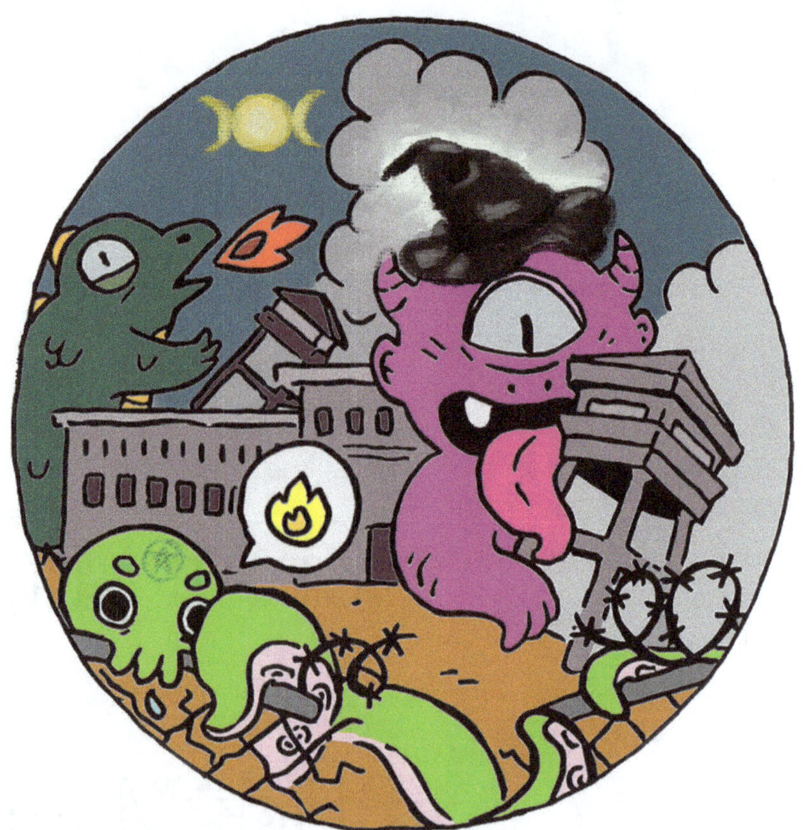

The A.B.O. Comix Collective is sustained by volunteers, community donations, grant funding, and various daring bank heists. It is also sustained by the perseverance, bravery, kindness, empathy, and love that our contributors share with us.

May our society learn to do no harm.

Edited by Casper Cendre, Brett Tomás Gonzalez
Cover art by Tammy Beth Graham
Back art by Raven Rodriguez

Library of Congress Control Number: 2026933382
ISBN-13: 978-1-961682-10-8

P.O. Box 11584, Oakland CA 94611 - abocomix@gmail.com

We speak as one, our minds unite,

The Lady and Lord we now invite.

By mysterious Moon and shining Sun,

There is magickal work to be done.

As we perform our Wiccan rite,

Goddess and God please add your Light.

Please guide us as you have before,

And empower our ritual once more.

Thank you for joining us at this time,

As we call to you with sacred rhyme.

HAIL AND WELCOME

-Spark Dalmatian

Table of Contents

A.B.O. Comix is an artist collective and small press supporting LGBTQ+ people surviving the prison industrial complex. We center the voices of imprisoned queer and trans creators by publishing their art, writing, and stories in anthologies like this one. All donations and proceeds from our books go towards commissary & art supplies, legal/parole/re-entry support, and other mutual aid. We maintain ongoing penpal relationships and advocacy for our friends inside, while operating an outside abolitionist collective to bridge the gap between prison walls and the outside world.

Throughout recorded history, accusations of witchcraft have often been used as a tool of social control, targeting those on the margins of society, those who dared to be different. In Europe and colonial America, witch trials led to imprisonment, torture, and executions, often with little or no evidence. While the methods have changed, the pattern of punishing people for defying social, religious, or gender norms continues today. In the modern U.S. prison system, many incarcerated people who practice pagan or earth-based religions still face harassment & discrimination, lack of access to religious materials, or outright bans on their spiritual practices. This anthology exists in part to bear witness to that ongoing resistance and survival.

A Caution to our readers. The intention of this book is to provide an opportunity for our brilliant community to describe what is meaningful for them. While we are constantly amazed by the wisdom of our authors and artists, we do not endorse any specific spiritual beliefs or practices. As with ANY spiritual practices, there are risks and rewards that must be weighed by the individual practitioner before beginning something new.

Editor's Note

I spent fourteen years inside, and in that time I crossed paths with people whose faiths and beliefs stretched in every direction. Sitting with them, surviving with them, letting our lives overlap day after day reshaped me in ways I still carry with gratitude. I am not Wiccan myself, but many of my closest friends were, especially within our little corner of the inside world. Their rituals and stories, their ways of marking intention, became part of the air around us, part of the language we used to hold each other up.

Toward the end of my sentence, thanks to the nature of the federal prison system, there was only one small doorway that meant hope for getting out early. We all had to serve at least eighty-five percent of our time, no real exceptions, unless we qualified for the Residential Drug Abuse Program that could shave a year off our sentence. On paper I qualified but anyone who has lived inside knows that what is written down and what actually happens can be two very different things. That year felt like something made of smoke, something I might reach for and watch slip through my fingers.

I was terrified walking into the interview with the DAP coordinator. I didn't know what would be asked, or whether the system would hold up its end. So I turned to the thing that had carried me through everything: community. I walked from friend to friend, looking for support, the way we all did when we were standing at one of those moments that could break you open either way. That closeness is something I still miss. Just being able to take a few steps and find someone who was living the same storm you were living.

One of the people I turned to was my friend Cubby. Now, Cubby insisted he was a cub, though the rest of us lovingly pointed out that he was very much an otter with an appetite for bears. But as confused as he might have been at his own otterness, he was absolutely steadfast on his Wiccan practices and beliefs. When I told him what I was facing, he didn't hesitate. He sat with me, talked with me, and then began to draw a set of symbols that meant something powerful to him. He sketched them onto a slip of paper, and we spent time talking through the intention behind them, settling our focus into the lines and shapes until they felt charged with something steady. I didn't know the full spiritual mechanics of what those symbols meant, but I understood the love and trust behind them.

I folded that paper and kept it in my pocket when I walked into the interview. And even though I was scared, I felt held. When they told me I wasn't eligible, something in me stayed calm. I didn't argue out of anger; I just spoke clearly about why they were wrong. And somehow, unbelievably, they listened. They corrected themselves. And I walked out with acceptance into the program that could give me a year of freedom.

I wish I could tell Cubby how I still think of that moment. I wish I could tell all my friends inside about the life I'm building and the strange, beautiful twist of fate that has me helping edit and design a Wicca anthology. I am currently prohibited from communicating with them but if I could, they would roll their eyes so hard at the idea that I'm the one doing this! And I know deep down they would jump at the chance to be in my shoes. I wish they were free beside me, creating and shaping this book in their own ways.

But they are not out here with me, so I do this with them in my heart. With their faces, their symbols, their laughter. With the memory of the ways we held each other up in a place that tried so hard to take our sense of meaning away. This note is simply my way of honoring them, and honoring the community whose voices fill these pages, with as much care and love as I can offer.

In Gratitude,
Brett Tomás Gonzalez

Introduction

I am not a witch…I just have one carved into my flesh.

Okay, so I live in a spooky haunted house with black walls and flickering candelabras. I have two cat familiars: one black, one attack-tabby (currently perched on my chair like a gargoyle, presumably guarding me from evil). Last night I cooked pasta in a cauldron while sipping on the blood of our good Lord—Merlot, they call it these days. There are dried herbs wrapped in twine smoldering in the corners, and encouraging spells (aka chalk graffiti) scrawled across every inch of the gallery. We currently have a Halloween-themed art show up. The book of Magic and Curses sits just out of reach on the top shelf of our abolitionist bookstore, right behind the jar of small animal bones.

Clearly, I've adopted the witch aesthetic.

So no, I may not be a witch, but I certainly know many. Since primary school, they've been my beloveds, my Muses, my fiercest alliances. One Valentine's Day in middle school, my two best friends and I dressed up in black gothic attire à la The Craft and crashed the school dance. I had a rolling backpack (uncool AF) and a pentagram necklace.

I've always felt a little less-than at home in my skin: the whole trans thing. But my witchy friends helped me decorate it, to feel just a little better in this flesh prison. We went to Hot Topic and dyed my hair bright red (a bit abnormal in 90s San Diego middle schools). We learned how to pierce ourselves and test the edges of our pain tolerance. They taught me emotional depth; how strong we are by how much we can endure. The first girl I ever kissed (more beautiful than Fairuza Balk, with snakebite piercings and a two-toned Chelsea haircut) bought me a book on witches so I'd "cool it with the Jesus shit."

To say witches haven't influenced the course of my life would be to deny the magic that's shaped it. I've been cursed at times, and no doubt, I probably deserved it. But my friends have also broken those curses, cast out the evil, and had my back when other pissed-off witches came for me.

Those who practice are no strangers to persecution. Those who know this planet holds magic and don't deny it—we now find them in prisons, instead of asylums or burned at the stake. But I don't think people so much deny that there's magic in the world; they just prefer it under a different name. (Science being a popular alternative.) (Ooh, edgy.)

Witchcraft can be dangerous. I'm quite accustomed to paranormal infestations: currently hosting a plague of flies resistant to modern extermination methods. But every practitioner has different aspirations, as every person is unique. Practice with caution and discernment, always, but magic comes alive when you believe in it. The mind is made of magic: it's full of dreams and the power to make those dreams real.

I'm grateful to our friends inside who've shared their experiences here. You've helped me better understand the mysteries of this world. Thank you for your glitter and grave dirt. May you be blessed.

In shadow and solidarity,
Casper Cendre the Co-Conspirator
Transcendent Liberator of Ideas & Images
and Patron Saint of Art as Abolition
(so sayeth the Sisters of Perpetual Indulgence)

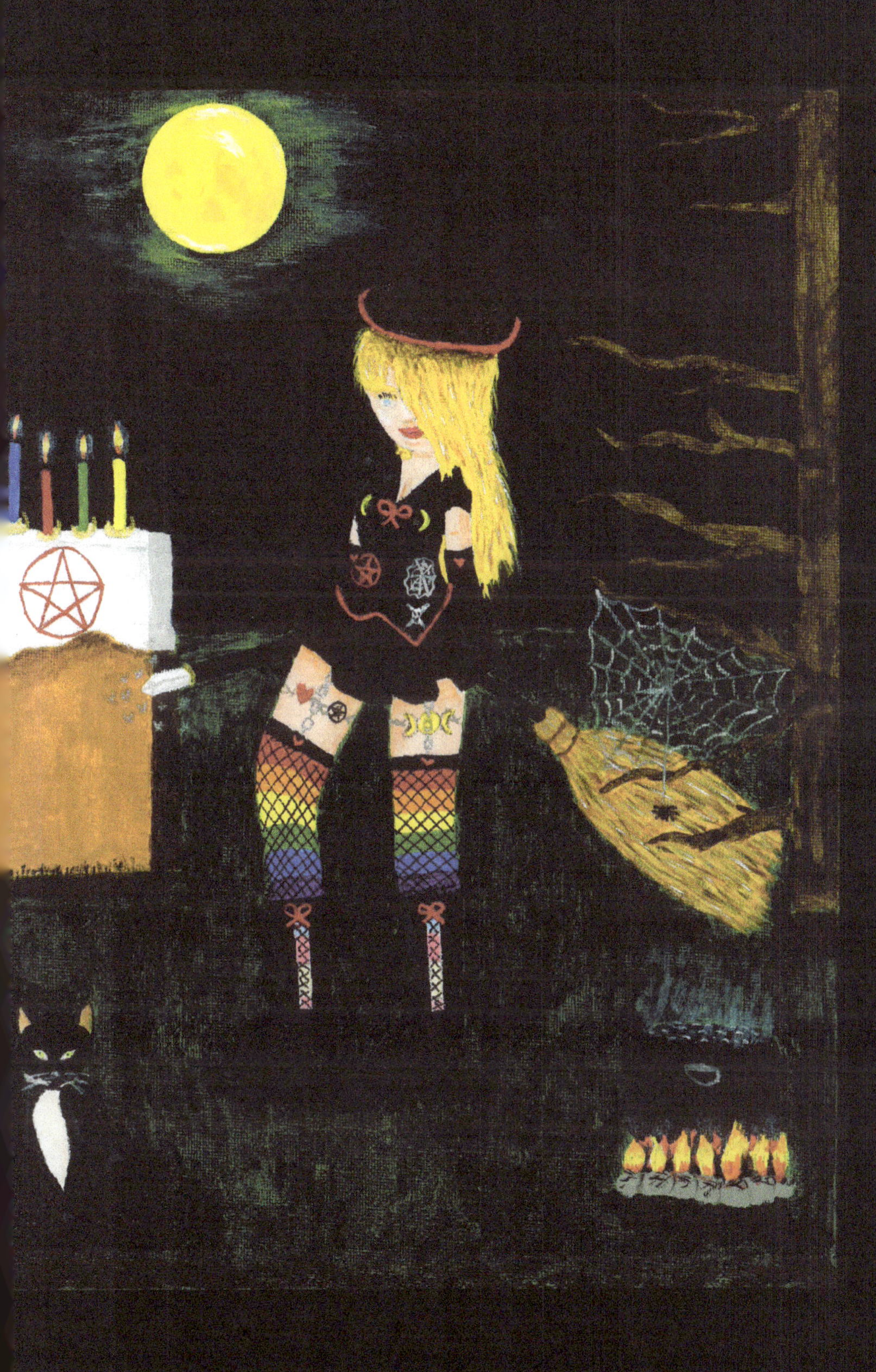

Starting a Religion in Prison
by Dennis "Abbadunamis" Mintun

When I first came to prison - twenty years ago - I was a very dedicated Christian. Of course, I was of the "if you do something wrong, repent, and you'll be okay" variety. Twenty years before that, I had even attended Bible college, and had been a junior pastor in a couple churches. Part of that time, you'd say I was a bona-fide "holy roller." But, I had a few issues. Okay... I had a lot of issues.

One of the biggest ones was that, for most of my life, I was "secretly" gay. Belonging to the Pentecostal Church of God, being homosexual was about the worst sin you could commit. I began to come out after my boy-friend, the senior pastor's son, told me I was a hypocrite. This was the morn-ing after I had preached on the "Sins of Sodom," and let people know how evil it was for a man to lie with a man. My boyfriend told me this as I woke up next to him, after a night of...

After that, I decided to "come out" - to a degree. It would still be years before I told most of my family - a very conservative Christian crowd, with only a few exceptions. From the pulpit, I announced that we should be tolerant of those of different sexual orientations. The next day, I was told I couldn't preach any more.

Eventually, I found the Metropolitan Christian Church. The MCC is pri-marily run by - and attended by - gays and transgenders. It was all right. But, since it was a lot closer to Lutheran than Pentecostal, I always felt a little out of place. I also began to question my religion, in other areas. I started thinking about some of the stories my grandfather told me when I was growing up about an old religion his ancestors had been part of, called "Erosian."

I also remembered an incident that had happened to me when I was seven. I'd gotten into trouble, and was on my bed, crying, when a bright light appeared in an upper corner of the room, and a voice spoke to me. I didn't really understand it, at the time. I never was sure if it was a dream, or if God was talking to me. All I know is the voice said, "I have called you, my Prince, to share love with a world that has forgotten what love is; to restore freedom to those who don't know they are bound; and to bring true joy back to a world that only pretends to be happy. For the next forty years, you will endure many hardships; sorrows; and times of loneliness. You will have few who will call you 'friend,' and, eventually, even your family will forsake you. You will have a hunger and a thirst to explore and experience every aspect of human nature. Through all, you will learn to love and understand the human race. At the end of forty years, you will have a time of intense spiritual training from various beings - human and otherwise - preparing for a time of victory and joy beyond your imagination. I call you 'Prince,' for you were born to be a king."

That incident was so profound that I never forgot it, although I did pretty much put it in the back of my mind, until many years later. After I'd been in prison for a few years, I remembered many of the stories Grandpa had told me. Stories about our ancestor, Alexander the Great; stories about various Greek gods; and how Queen Aphrodite had made her consort, Eros, King after her. Even stories about ancient Atlantis. But, those, too, I put in the back of my mind.

Upon my arrival in prison, one of the first things I did was get involved in the chapel's "Open Fellowship" - a non-denominational Christian service run by the inmates every Sunday. Because I love to sing, I became heavily involved with the choir. Eventually, I became part of the "Set-Up Committee" that decided what we were going to do each week.

Then, one day, the inmate who was the primary preacher, "Monty," taught a familiar sermon… on the "sins of Sodom." After the service, I pulled Monty aside and told him that I disagreed with what he had said. Point blank, he asked me if I was gay. When I told him I was, he told me I couldn't participate in the choir or the committee any longer. The chaplain upheld Monty's decision. So, I stopped going to the chapel.

One day, a former drag queen that everyone called "Granny" was talking to me. He told me he was Wiccan, and invited me to attend a Wiccan meeting. I'd always been taught Wiccans were Satanists, so was afraid to go. Finally, Granny talked me into it. Sure enough, at the service, they prayed to "the horned one!" I later found out they were referring to their god Cernunnos, who was represented by a horned stag. They didn't even believe in Satan. For awhile, I attended Wiccan services. I even became part of the leadership. In some ways, this religion felt good. But, it wasn't exactly right. I still considered myself a Christian, in a sense. I even called myself a "Christian Wiccan."

Since I had a lot of time on my hands, I began to study the Bible in earnest. Not like I'd been taught - but actually learning ancient Greek and studying what it actually said. I also studied other religions, including many of the ancient Greek sects. They "felt" like they were sort of what I was looking for.

Then came June sixth of 2006 (or 6/6/06). I was put in the "hole" for sexual activity that a friend and I had engaged in six months prior. In protest, I began a hunger strike. Nobody noticed. After about three days, my hunger strike turned into a religious fast. I decided to use it to try and find out what the "right" religion was for me. My fast lasted for ten days. Then, I once again heard a voice speak to me. Some claim it may have been a delusion due to my prolonged fast, or something else. I choose to believe it was who he said it was…the god Eros. The voice said: "My child; my heir. Fruit of my loins. It is time to pick up the mantle that you have been preparing for. I've called you 'prince' - now I call you 'king.' It is time for you to gather your subjects. The kingdom is the 'Kingdom of Erotes' - Erotes being the name for all the gods and goddesses who follow me, Eros. Your name shall be 'Abbaduna-mis-Eros-Alexandros te Arcturus Whitelion d'Erotes.' This name will give you and others a clue as to your station, your heritage, and your destiny."

Since it was Eros, and since there was some similarity to what I was told and what my grandfather had told me of the ancient religion, I began to write down everything I could remember about his stories. I also did a lot of meditation - writing down every thought and image that came to me.

When I finally got out of the hole, I made a proposal to the prison chapel team to begin a new religion. At first, because I figured it would get approved easier, I called it "Greek Wiccan." When it did get approved, there were some hurt feelings from Granny and the Celtic Wiccan group…who changed their name to "Eclectic Wiccan."

My group took off like gangbusters. I taught what little I knew, using the Wiccan format for rituals and ceremonies. My grandfather had long been gone, but a cousin of mine helped find any information he could on the Erosian path. There wasn't much. Even online, it was fairly well unknown. Then, the dam burst, and I received all sorts of information from various sources. One major source was a box of notes and rituals that my cousin found that had belonged to my grandfather. Since almost our whole family were Christian, he had kept it well-hidden. My cousin thought, since the religion had been pretty much a secret from the world, maybe it should stay that way. I disagreed, largely because of what I believed Eros had told me. To see if I was on the right path, I outlined two types of classes for my chapel group to vote on. I proposed: 1) Greek Wicca, run similar to other Wiccan groups, with me as High Priest; or 2) The Erosian Path - essentially re-founding the ancient religion, with me as King. There were over forty people there to vote. Only two voted for the first choice. Everyone else thought that the Erosian path needed to be made into a "new" religion.

It's been a long, uphill battle. I've often had to fight with prison administration about my religion. Fortunately, because Idaho (where I am) has a large Mormon population, freedom of religion is a very important part of the state constitution - probably stronger than the federal constitution. We now have a good, firm foothold. As people leave prison, they take our religion with them. To me, it's the right thing. The Erosian path teaches the premise of "do no harm, except to protect yourself and loved ones," as well as the "Four Pillars"...

- Love (and acceptance) of all people, places, things, and concepts
- Joy in all circumstances; finding the good in everything
- Freedom for all people - body, soul and mind
- Magecraft ("Magic"). The manipulation of energy. Basically, science that has not yet been explained

I know these principles have helped inmates to be better, more tolerant people. I know that humankind needs these principles. It hasn't been easy starting a religion up that has been pretty much unheard of for a couple thousand years. But, I believe with all my heart that I am doing what I am supposed to be doing.

At least I am accomplishing something with my time. Most people in prison tend to "spin their wheels," or even just drift through the days.

Believe me. I am definitely no saint. The only reason I'm the leader is because nobody else was. Maybe I'm completely "off the wall." Maybe I have delusions of grandeur. Maybe. Maybe not. Maybe, I came to prison in order to "steer" me in the right direction.

It sure was a winding path!

An Amazon Prayer

i'm lucky to be alive,
    tho' stuck in the Abyss
in this Hell on Earth
    called prisxn.
i've learned to thrive
    and faced my fear of Death.
i'm like a rainbow —
    a light seen thru a prism.
At first life was hard
    and i tended to make things worse.
Resisting injustices of captivity,
    i was beaten and tortured,
    i thought i was cursed.
Twenty-five years and counting,
    "Three Strikes" and i'm out!
No matter how i've changed
    or what comes about,
    they won't let me out!
i'm stressed and depressed,
    traumatized and oppressed,
been suicidal more than once,
    misgendered and politically repressed.
when i "came out" as trans/queer,
    i walked the yard with pride,
i found Love and Hope again,
    and determined never to hide
    my true Self — an Amazon!
At times i'm lonely and sad,
    thinking of the life i've missed;
but Life itself is beautiful,
    and i know it's better than this!
The Struggle has made me stronger,
    so no matter what happens,
no matter how much longer,
    i thank Goddess for Her blessings.

An Amazon prayer:
    O Goddess Hecate Dark Moon,
Mistress of the Crossroads to Hell;
    Please show me the right path
    so i may prosper and be well!

- jennifer amelia rose

Prayer of Protection
by Jeffery Lewis Dukes aka Déz

Hi Family – A.B.O. Comix

Blessed Be! This is your Brother Jefferey. I received my Newsletter #7 and enjoy every one I read. Please forgive me for not writing sooner, I've been working and preparing myself for getting out next year in March so I ask for your prayers and good energy.

In your opportunities theres a request for "contribute to a book on Wicca practice in prison." I've been a Wiccan since 2013. A very good friend named "Cat" who became my wife/relationship partner – she was a sweet partner/Transgender, she's out of prison -- Thank it be to Goddess Hekate. Well we was in Ad-Seg one time and she began to meditate and raise energy. I felt the power in the cell and I ask how I can do that. So she got serious and asked if I was truthful. I said so -- Yes. She taught me the prayer of Oath which I prayed and ever since I have been studying and practicing Wicca. Even though we're not together anymore but she's my spiritual Mother in the faith.

I have a prayer I wish to share to all that is willing to say it. It's one of Protection:

"Hekas, Hekas Este Be-Beloi"

Waxing, waxing, growing, growing Hekate power is flowing, flowing: Oh gracious Lady, day and night Protect us by your holy might; For thrice around this Circles bound all evil energy stick into the ground.

From the heavens above to the earth below Send your power down below. Air, fire, water, earth Souls of men, hearts of woman evil flees Stars of power, point aflame in the unity of Goddess name. I move outside the limits of time to work this spell of mine. All Elements energy weaves the universe in time exist by my desire and will, tide this Magick unto Me. So mote it be. Blessed Be.

Scrying with Water
by janetter xoxo

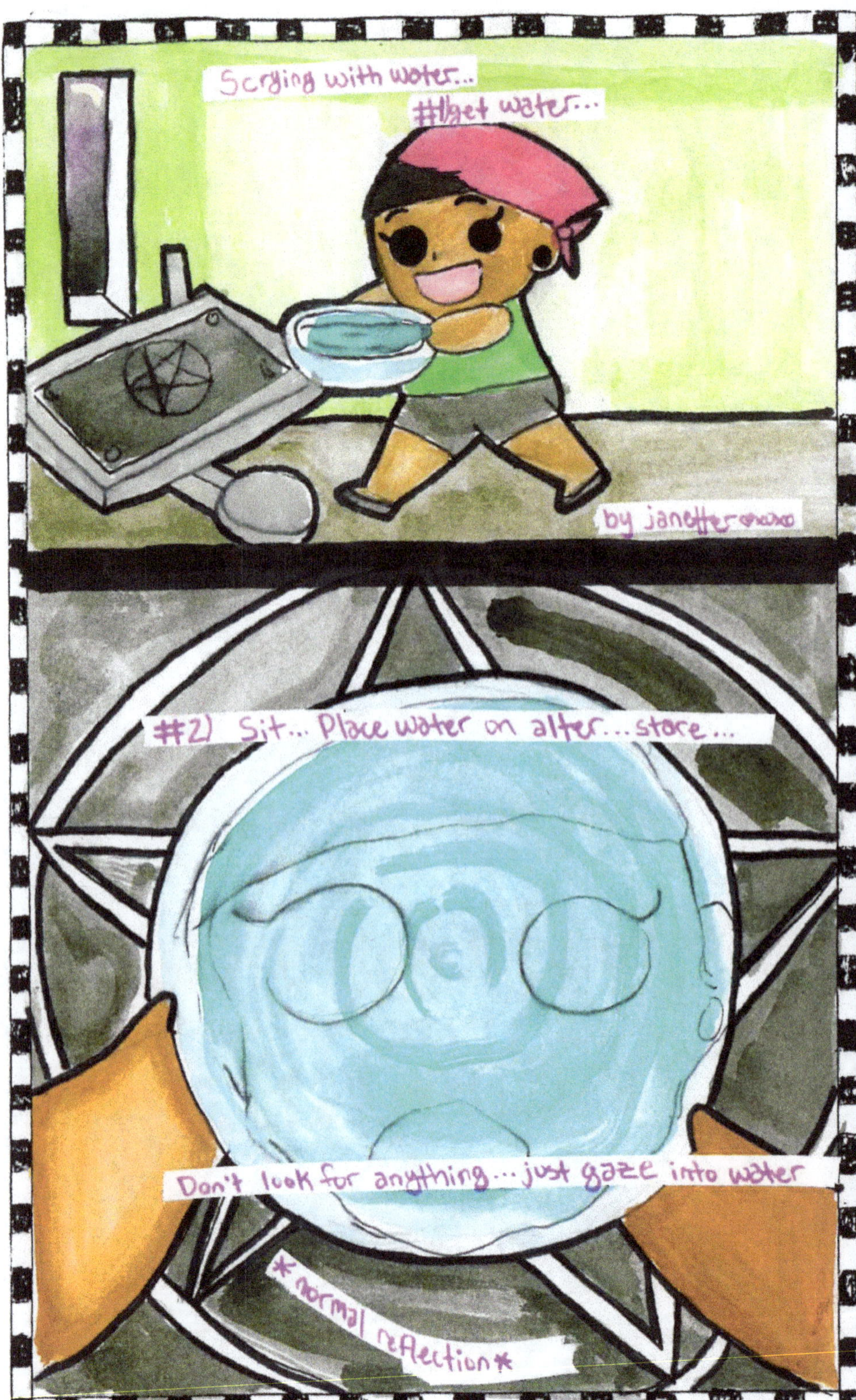
Scrying with water...
#tibet water...
by janette xoxo
#2) Sit... Place water on alter... store...
Don't look for anything... just gaze into water
* normal reflection *

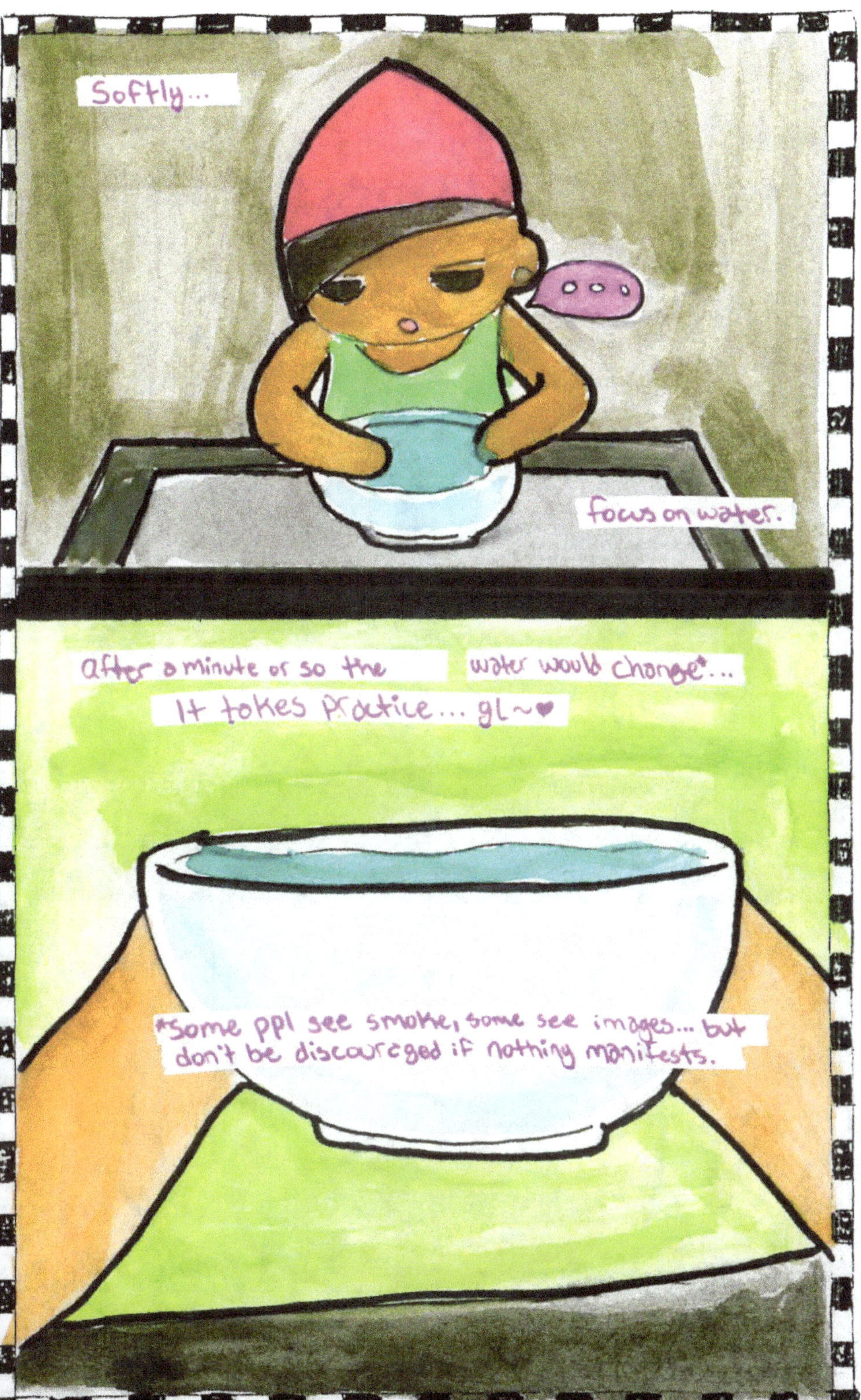

Softly...
focus on water.
after a minute or so the water would change*...
It tokes practice... gl~♥
*Some ppl see smoke, some see images... but don't be discouraged if nothing manifests.

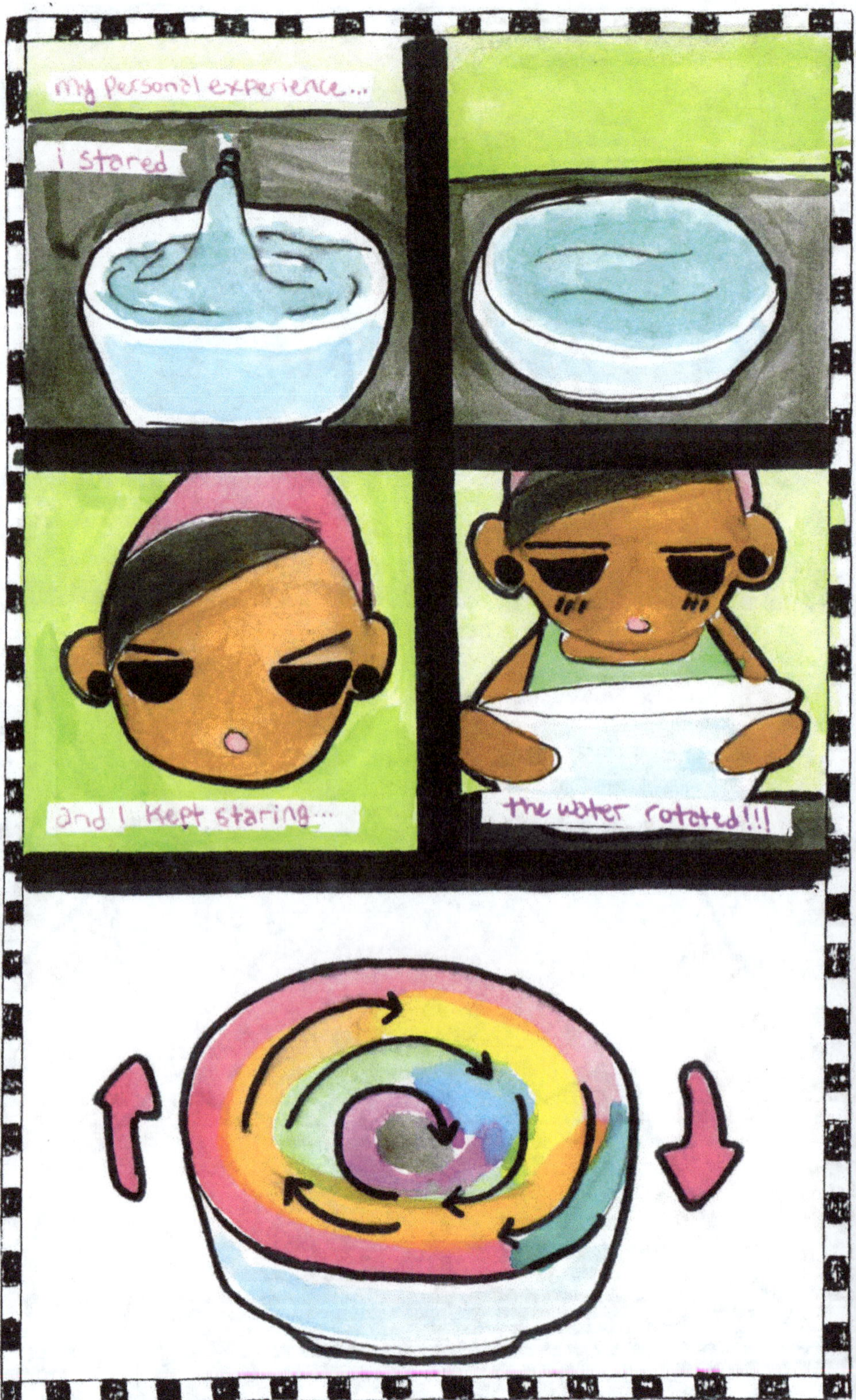
my personal experience...
i stared
and i kept staring...
the water rotated!!!

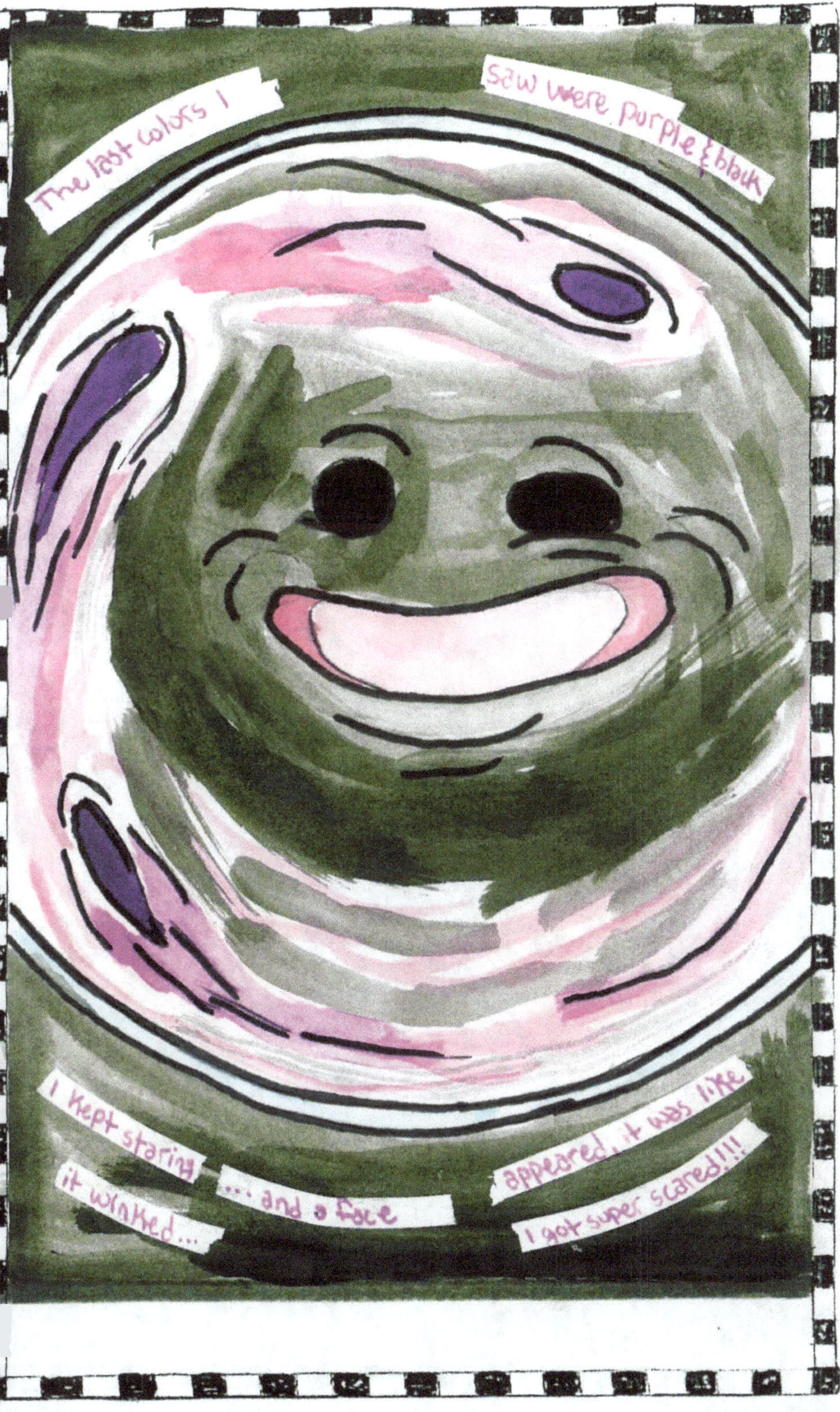
The last colors I
saw were purple & black
I kept staring
it winked...
...and a face
appeared, it was like
I got super scared!!!

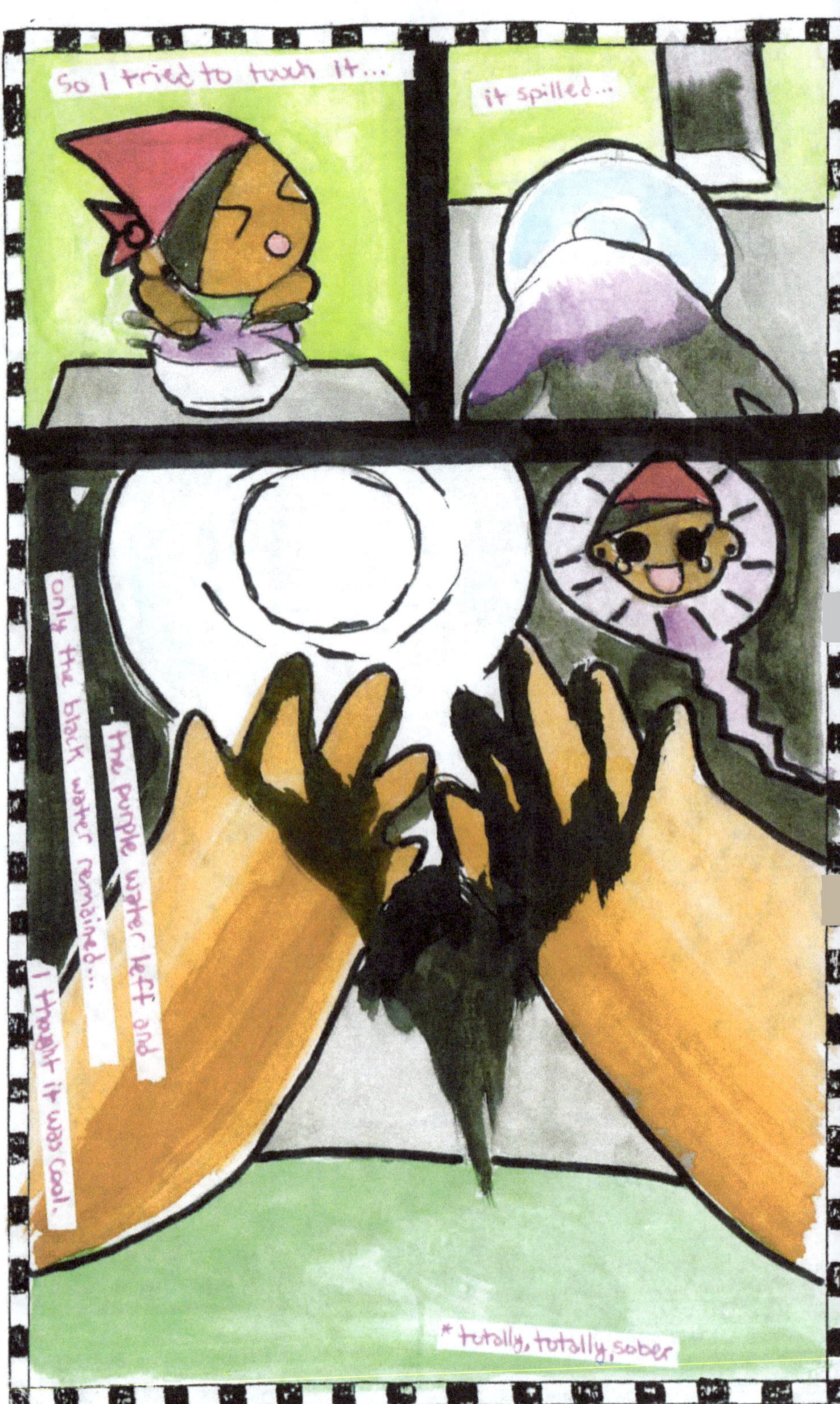
So I tried to touch it...
it spilled...
only the black water remained...
the purple water left and
I thought it was cool.
* totally, totally, sober

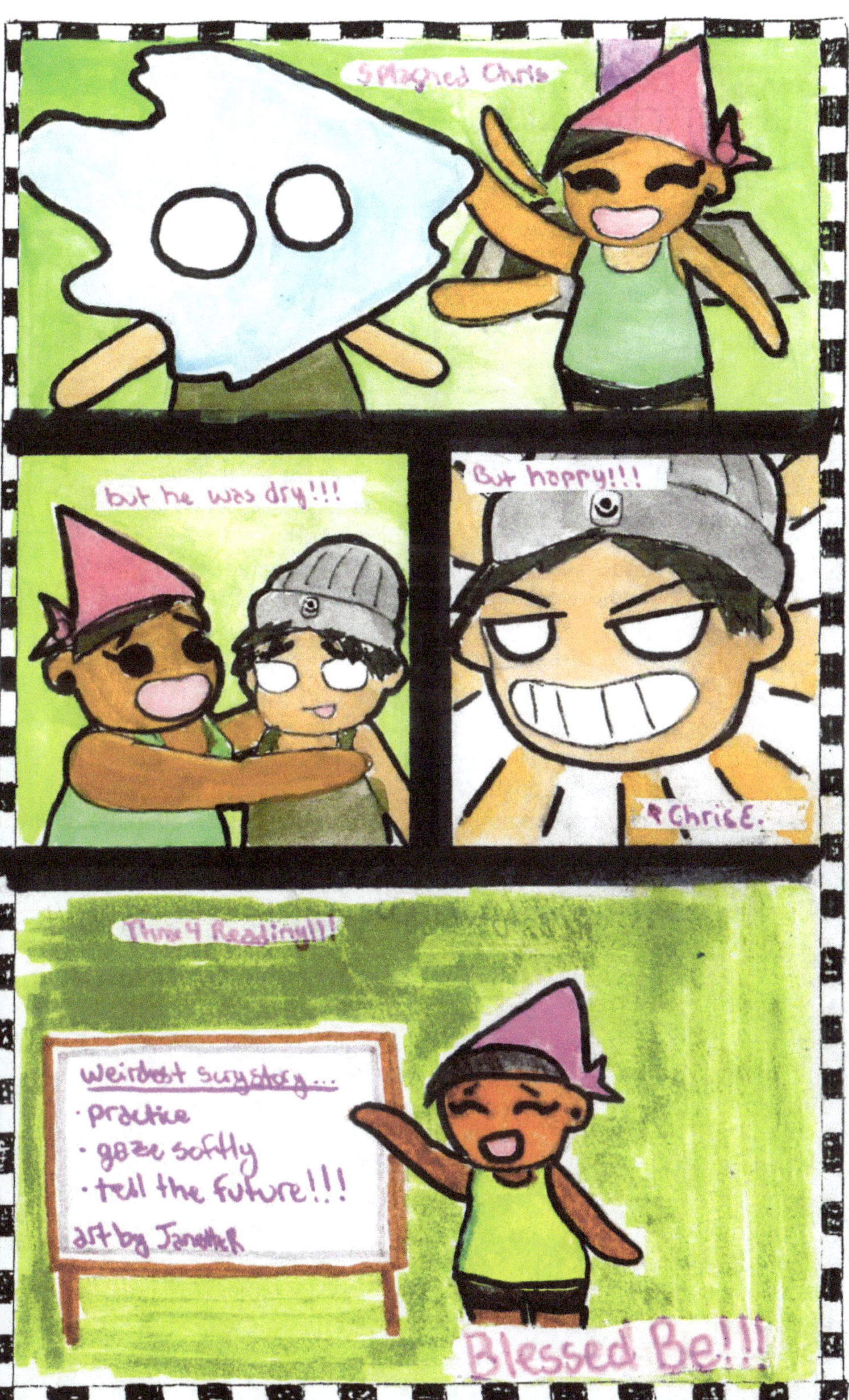
Splashed Chris
but he was dry!!!
But happy!!!
& Chris E.
Thnx 4 Reading!!!
Weirdest scrystory...
· practice
· gaze softly
· tell the future!!!
art by Janathan
Blessed Be!!!

The Witch's Craft
by Samantha Dynamite

Magic is the ability to make life conform to ones own will power. This is no written rule, it is my own self experience by using the tenets to practice magic. I am Pagan, not by choice. I AM Pagan because it is what has always been natural to me. Pagan meaning, a practitioner of the ancient ways of being in union with Nature and what comes Naturally. I embrace many written Laws of Wicca. But I have adopted all aspects of Witch Craft. In my lives I have come to realize that everyone alive is endowed with magic. Only those of us who do not run from the challenge of discovering that magics ability to transform us is worthy of its many gifts bestowed. Magics story is the time tested story of LOVE. In the flesh we are incomplete. Our Soul has lost its memory and it is our task to help it remember its Self so that we can wed the Flesh with its Spirit and wake up the Magic. We mourn this fracture in all that we do until we decide to do something about it. The Quest is us doing the work to unite our two halves. We seek this union in external ways. Sex, drugs, thrills, money, etc. But none of these can compare to the reunion of You with Yourself. Each step toward the Self brings the powers Magic is said to confer. The whole Universe reaches out to teach us the way back to our Godness. It is my experience that we all must take this journey, regardless what Spiritual belief one has. The day that I remembered my Soul I cried uncontrollably. I became unable to lie to myself anymore. Nor could any one else lie to me. It is the ability to KNOW. Witch Craft makes one "Knowing." In my incarceration I find this time my college in further knowing that magic of which I am made of. That everything is made of! This knowledge swallows the fear of Death and the end of all Things. Because magic marries everything in existence into infinite bliss. When my time comes to shed this illusion called flesh, I will do so proudly having emerged from this cocoon of humanity into the ethereal continuance of the Butterfly called Me. I AM Magic. And so are You. Your Quest is Noble. Honor the God and Goddess within. No failure exists on this Path of the Lovers Heart. If this were not so, the World as we know it would cease to exist. And as we all well know: We Are All Still Here! Blessed Be Ye.

A Spell Of Empowerment to find the Self in You.

Always remember that Witches are natural magicians. Ceremonial Magic is used with the help of God forms or by calling on Divine or Infernal beings. There is no such thing as Good or Bad Magic. Only that which you yourself intends determines if the result is set to either a Good or Bad end.

This Spell will help one awaken their own Divine Guardian so that they may be taught True magic from the One in which the source of magic within is derived.

Take a bowl of cold water, half filled. Spit in it. Swirl the water around 7 times with your right pointer finger.

While doing so Chant: "Water mirror wild and free, show my Divine Guardian to me." Do this Three times.

Then stand near or under a light and look into the water at your reflection. Blow on the water by breathing in deeply, hold it, then blow out slowly. You have now charged the water with your own energy, made it alive by your spit, purified it with your finger to destroy all deception. And spoken Words of Power into its substance. This is True Magic.

Stare into the water when it is still and only look into your eyes.

When you are confident you are staring into the eyes. They will not be Your Eyes but that of your Divine Guardian. Near you have a pen and some paper handy. Write down everything that comes to your mind. Scribble any symbols. Keep making eye contact for long periods with the reflection you see. Then speak this Invocation: "Whispered voices in the wind, unleash my Divine Guardian within!" Do this for no more then an hour and a half. At the conclusion of this spell to The Divine Self, praise what ever God and Goddess that you worship. If you've not chosen a particular God or Goddess, say: "Oh Blessed Mother of Nature. Bright and shining Morning Star. Your peace, love, and favor I covet. My Horned and Wild Father of every Forest. Protect and guide me in these magic endeavors as you would my feet in the thrill of the Hunt. This bowl be my Body. This Water be my Blood. I pour it out onto you as my libation for it to be a favorable sacrifice to You. So Note it Be!"

It is good to pour this water on grass or soil of the ground. If you can not. It should be half drank and half poured down a drain.

The power of this spell increases the more you use it. It will give you the power of Clairvoyance and the ability to hear the voice of your Guardian so as to always be wisely instructed. No false words or ill guidance can your Divine Guardian give because it is your Highest Brilliant Self. To all who use this Spell, be ye blessed!

How I thrive in practicing Magic in Prison. A Poem.

There are many ways I grow my knowledge and hone my practice of the Craft behind bars. I instead of being under the open sky I imagine that I'm the stars.

My paint brush is my Wand. And my bunk mat is my broom. Every time I close my eyes I disappear from my room.

AbRaCaDaBrA! I am reborn. A phoenix on the thermal winds or the breeze riding a Thunder storm.
I invoke the Goddess and force myself to be honest.
I curse those that curse us.
And bless those who keep their promise.
My only promise is to: Do what I Will.
As long as it hurts no one, I will do what I Feel.
And Magic bleeds from my pores like a perfect perfume.
Love, Lust, and Let it Be, permeates my room.
No steel bars, or handcuffs can tie these hands up.
Being a Witch means you're tough, I say the word and my Gods show up.
I cast the Circle, summon the Guardians of the four Watch Towers, and erect my cone.
Anywhere there is passion, practice, and like-minded people around.
I AM HOME.
And whenever I'm alone I hear my Sisters prayers in the Wind.
Prison can not limit the Temple from Within.
Blessed Be, my Friends!

::Written by: Lady Queen Samantha PenDragon. The Queen of Hearts
<3/ <3/ <3
The Goddess of All Elves. 11/11/11

Magickal Runes. Scripts.
ᛗᚱᚷᛁᚻᚱᛚ ᛡᚼᛏᚠᛋ ᛋᚻᚱᛁᚴᛏᛋ

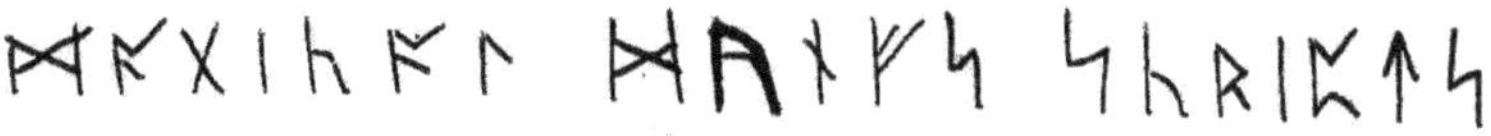

And Alphabets.
ᚱᛏ� ᚠᛚᚴᚻᚠᛒᛗᛏᛋ

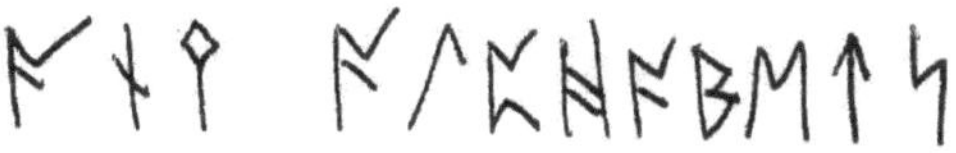

A Historic View of PEGAN
Fonts.

By TAMMY BETH GRAHAM
23[Rd] June, 2023

"Aleister Crowley: "Every intentional act is a magickal act"

when you have a strong "intention" and focus it ie. "Attention" you acomplish The first 2 parts of magick spell casting. Intent is what you want To be or to happen if you intend on 2 people to fall in Love. you will Need to focus such intent into you spell, talisman, or fetish.
Think of some of The childhood Rhymes you know "TammyBeth And John setting in a tree Kissing, first Comes, Love, Then Comes Marrage, The Tammy Beth with a Baby Carrage." This is in it-self a spell The intent is That I TammyBeth fall in Love, Marry and have Johns Baby. intent, focus. when you Repeat it over and over you infact focus you internal energies into The spell. Simple Love Magick.

Magick is the art of Creating Change in Accordance with your will. — Skye Alexander

Intent means determining your Objective and then Performing an action with awareness, consciously Channeling energy and emotion into the action in Order. to produce a given desired Result.

Remember when you Use emotions in the art of Spell work you need to take Caution Because your state of mind Can cause an undesired effect. in example if you are mad and try a Love spell. you may be able to bring two people together but your Anger is Now A part of that Love. you will doom The spell. too you should Know That Love and Hate are the two Strongest emotions.

Some folx when Casting a spell will try to ~~my~~ Make a Rhyme or Song of it. This is ok if it helps you focus and pour your energy into The spell.

Affirmations: are an easy form of magick. and I enjoy This form Just Keep them simple and from The Heart. Here is an example:

I am a Witch of a Kind Heart and My God/Goddess leads Me So Mote it be.

Some folx say blessed be, So be it, or So mote it be. You can Simply Say it is done all will woRk

Magick to Me is Not what most would except YEt it work. You Must find what works for you, I for one have a mixture of Native Amarican medicine Voodoo, Saxon with witch craft. and to top it of Some Catholic tradition. After all Jesus was a Hippy Nomad, That performed Magick and was Then Sacrificed of The Mount of The Skull! That s Some kinda power full. Some folx only Use Gods/Goddess of One Type ie. celtic, Germanic, Greek, Roman, etc I have many Loki is my favored He, she, and They. are fun a joker and Bring Joy to my life. I just use The Big Joker from a deck of cards on my alter to Repersent Them. I must explain Loki was Killed by his brother The God Thor. Then thor brought Loki Back as a Goddess. That was Thor playing his prank on Loki the God of pranks Laughes. I am very much a desendent of Loki for I joke often.

How ever I have others I pray to my ancestors which is a Native Amarican Traditional Medicen. I beat The drum and chant, I also have a host of other That I am fond of.

If you wish to Lean more about God/Goddess you Can get a copy of "The Oxford dictionary of World Mythology"

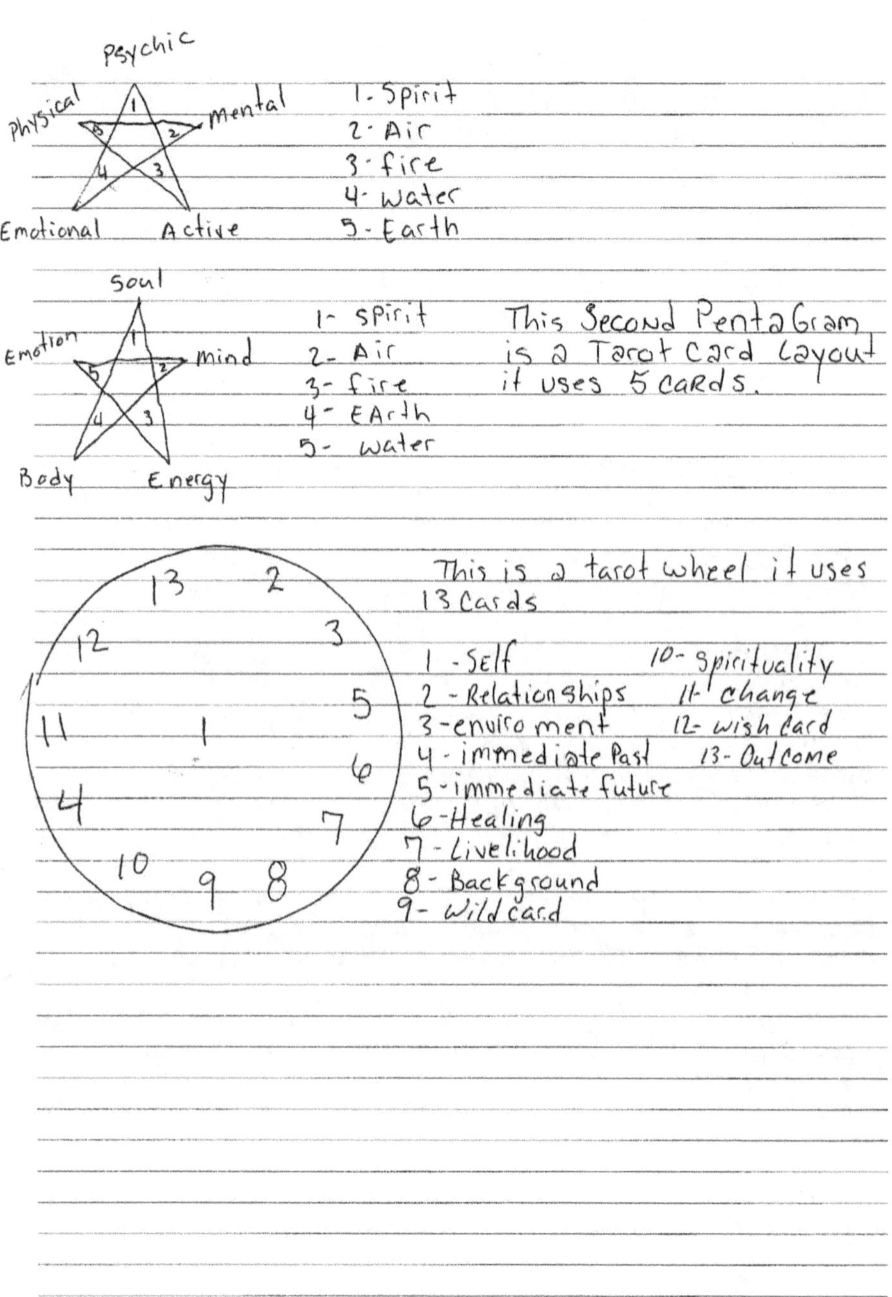

This Second PentaGram is a Tarot Card Layout it uses 5 cards.

This is a tarot wheel it uses 13 cards

1 - Self
2 - Relationships
3 - enviroment
4 - immediate Past
5 - immediate future
6 - Healing
7 - Livelihood
8 - Background
9 - Wild card
10 - Spirituality
11 - change
12 - wish card
13 - Outcome

ONDINE'S TREE of Life Tarot Layout

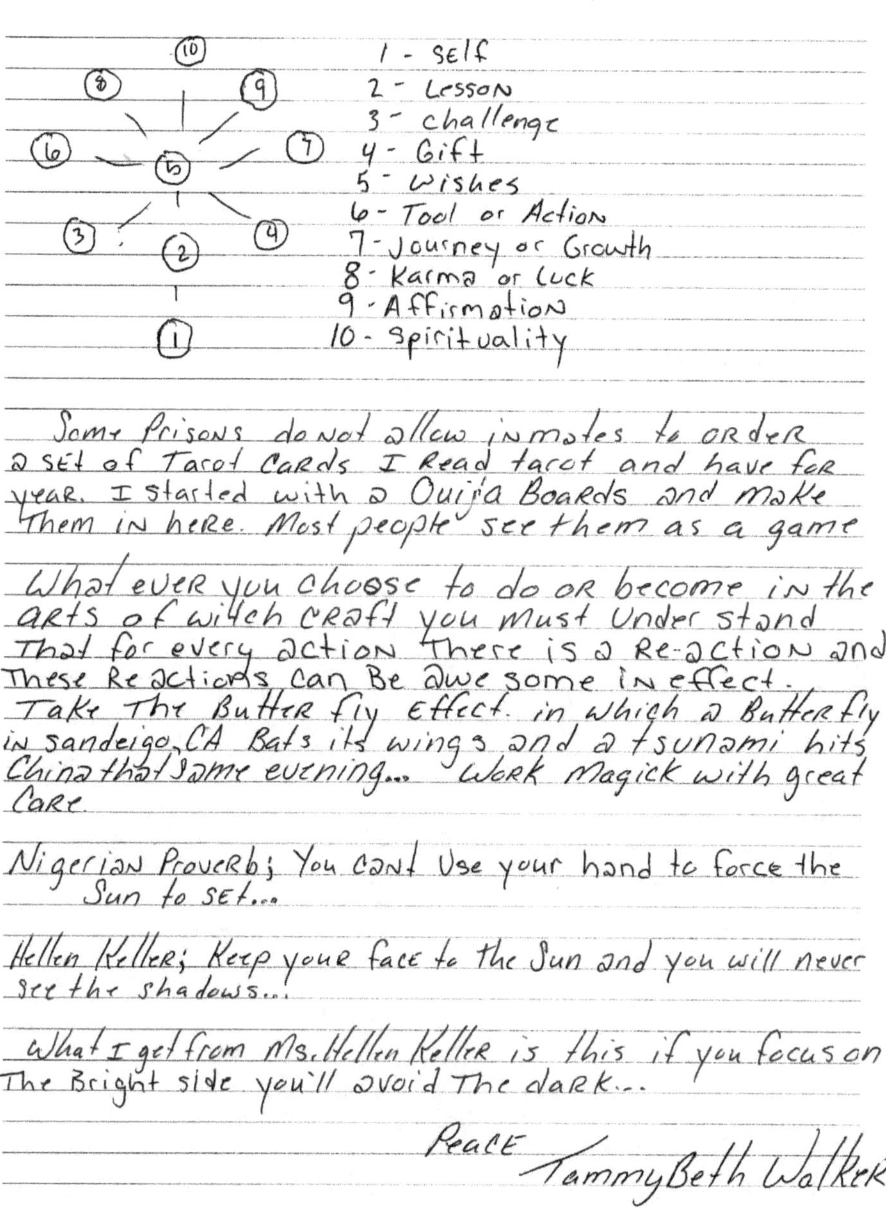

1 - Self
2 - Lesson
3 - challenge
4 - Gift
5 - Wishes
6 - Tool or Action
7 - Journey or Growth
8 - Karma or Luck
9 - Affirmation
10 - Spirituality

Some Prisons do not allow inmates to order a set of Tarot Cards I Read tarot and have for year. I started with a Ouija Boards and make Them in here. Most people see them as a game

Whatever you choose to do or become in the arts of witch craft you must Understand That for every action There is a Re-action and These Reactions can Be awesome in effect. Take The Butterfly effect. in which a Butterfly in sandeigo, CA Bats its wings and a tsunami hits China that Same evening... Work Magick with great Care.

Nigerian Proverb; You cant Use your hand to force the Sun to set...

Hellen Keller; Keep your face to the Sun and you will never see the shadows...

What I get from Ms. Hellen Keller is this if you focus on The Bright side you'll avoid The dark...

Peace
TammyBeth Walker

①

The Elder Futhark Runes

ᚠ - Fehu - Cattle. God Frey - Power and wealth

ᚢ - Uruz - Aurochs (wild Oxen) - Strength of will

ᚦ - Purisaz/Thurisaz - Giant God of Thor - Danger or Protection

ᚨ - Ansuz - The God of Odin - Prosperity, Vitality, Stability

ᚱ - Raidho - Ride/wheel - Focus, Movement, Work, Growth

ᚲ - Kenaz - Torch - Understanding, Learning, inspiration

ᚷ - Gebo - Gift - Generosity, Giving, And Receiving

ᚹ - Wunjo - Joy - Joy, Wellbeing, Good News

ᚺ - Hagalaz - Hail - Destruction, chaos

ᚾ - Naudhiz - Need - Need, Unfulfilled desire

ᛁ - Isaz/Isa - Ice - Waiting

ᛃ - Jera - Year, Harvest, Reward

ᛇ - Eihwaz - Yew - Strength, stability, endings, + Beginings

ᛈ - Perthro/Pertho - dice cup - Chance, Problem solving

ᛉ - Elhaz/Algiz - Elk or shield - Restraint, Protection from enemies

ᛊ - Sowila/Sowulo - Sun - Success, Solace

ᛏ - Tiwaz - The god of Tyr - Victory, honor, Success

ᛒ - Berkanan/Berkana - Birch - Fertility, Growth, sustenance, Begining

ᛖ - Ehwaz - horse - Trust, faith, Companionship

ᛗ - Mannaz - Man - Potential, Support

ᛚ - Laguz - water, Lake - formlessness, Unknown

ᛜ - Ingwaz/Inguz - The god Yngvi, Fertility, beginings, Potential

ᛟ - othalan/othala - inheritance/home - heritage, tradition.

ᛞ - Dagaz - Day - Hope + Happiness

②

German Futhark Runes

F	U	Th	A	R	K	G	W	H	N	I	J	Ë	P	Z	S	T

B	E	M	L	Ng	D	O

Saxon Futhorc Runes

F	U	Th	O	R	C	G	W	H	N	I	Gh	S	T	B	E	M	L

NG	OE	D	A	AE	Y	EA	K	V

Anglo-Saxon Runes

A	B	C	D	E	F	G	H	I	J	L	M	N	O	P	R	S	T	Ë	U

W	Y	Z	AE	EA	OE	NG	Th

During The midevil days Pegan's were on The Down Low due to Christian's trying to Kill Them. So To Pocess Copies of of Their Grimoire was such a Risk That They came up with Secret Runes to Hide Their macick

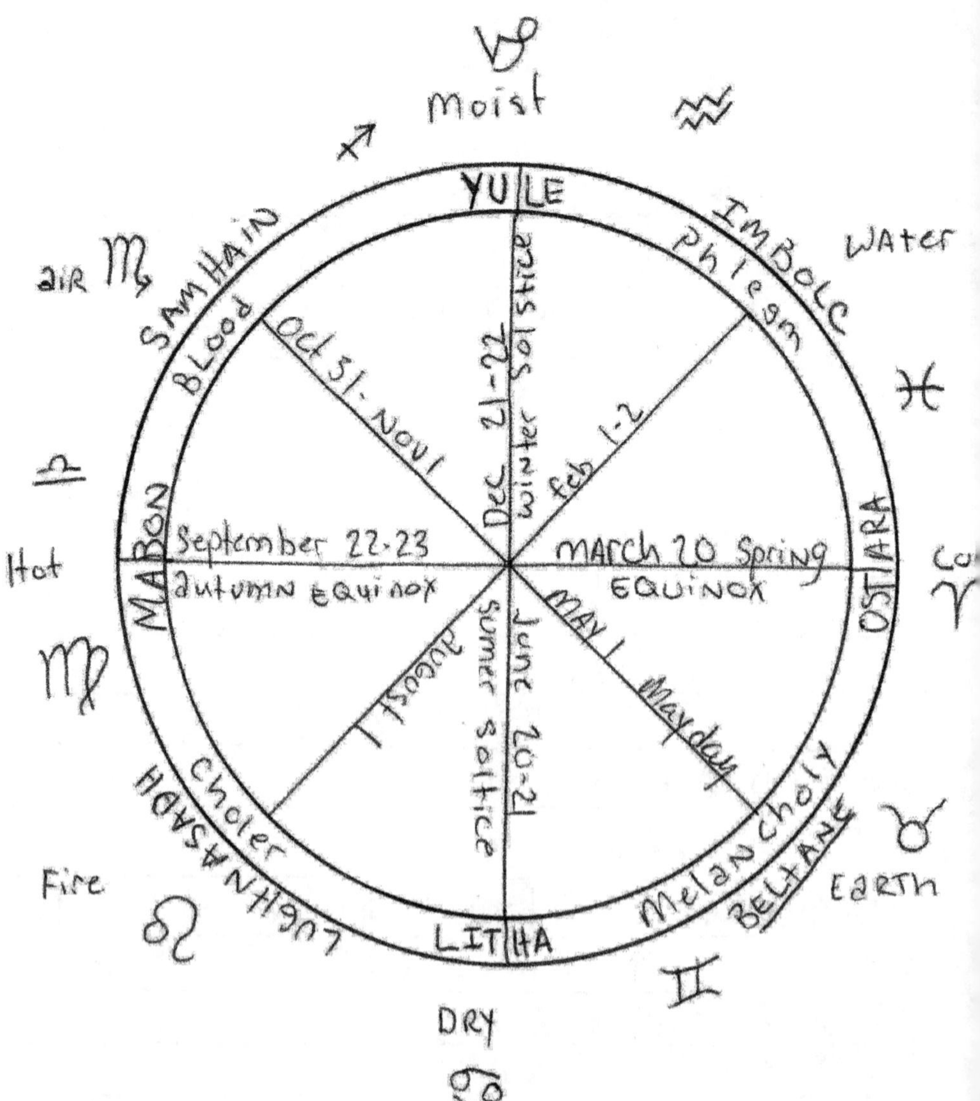

moist
air
Water
Hot
Fire
DRY
EARTH
YULE
IMBOLC
OSTIARA
BELTANE
LITHA
LUGHNASADH
MABON
SAMHAIN
Phlegm
Blood
Choler
Melancholy
September 22-23 autumn Equinox
march 20 Spring Equinox
Oct 31- Nov 1
Dec 21-22 winter solstice
Feb 1-2
May 1 Mayday
June 20-21 sumer soltice
August 1

(Charge of the Goddess)

This is the "Charge of the Goddess,"
my power is no longer sealed.
Through the sacred feminine of our coven,
my craft has now been revealed.
No longer will we be considered unworthy,
or anything less than a man.
Freedom, justice and equality,
seen through the wisdom, so you will understand.
That the word was with the Goddess,
and through the Goddess powerful words were spoken.
I will separate the light from the darkness,
and leave the creeds forever broken.
Cause the charge, is against you.
Who hated us, no matter how hard we would try.
The charge, is against you.
Who wanted to see the ancient feminine die.
Through the destruction, chaos and terror,
and the screams of those who were slain.
The universe has corrected its sin,
and the face of the Goddess will remain.

- Charlie Harbert

Practicing Paganism in Prison
by A.D. White

What a joy to not be a Christian! What a joy to love the Earth and cel-ebrate one's ancestors! How lovely to practice magic and be one's feminine self without a fear of condemnation! A pagan can feel free, even while con-fined, and the positive energy within attracts good things that make incar-cerated life more livable. Why doesn't everyone in here embrace paganism? I simply have no good answer to that question.

Two pagan prayers:

Praise be to our Mother Earth,
Full of beauty and magic.
Provider and sustainer,
To forget her would be tragic.

For loving her I feel no shame,
This healer of my soul.
Ertha is her ancient name,
In her presence I feel whole.

Frigga, please watch over me,
Keep me free from harm –
Queen of Asgard, I call on Thee

Mother Above, please never depart,
Let us walk together –
Mistress of Fensalir, I praise Thee

Spinner of clouds, please give me wings
So that my spirit can fly –

Soaring One, I honor Thee
Frigga, may I ever be
Your true and faithful child –
Blessed Mother, remember me

Andrea (My Feminine Self)

My name is Andrea, daughter of Thor,
And I follow the Northern way.
I'm still ablaze at forty-four –
I eat, I love, I pray.

I've walked the path of fire,
Felt my skin blister and char;
The flames just took me higher,
Now I shine like a star.

I sink deep into meditation
To find the secrets within.
I live with wonder, not trepidation –
Each day new adventures begin.

Two Spirits

Without warning or any plan, I was touched by the Feminine. To feel a whole new presence within oneself at age 40 is a surprising and jarring experience. I quickly embraced it though, and formally "invited" in the feminine spirit. It has been quite a ride since then, and I have to say I'm better for this occurrence. I'm stronger, wiser, and more loving. I'm less angry and agitated. I feel more whole. Prison is not the ideal place to experience such a thing, and to be such a person, but that is outside of my control.

Where does Andrew end and Andrea begin, and who's running the show? I don't know, and I'm fine with that! It is a fuller life, and it is a less mundane life. I'm not like the other guys here, but that's okay. As the mom says in The Craft: Legacy, "Your difference is your power."

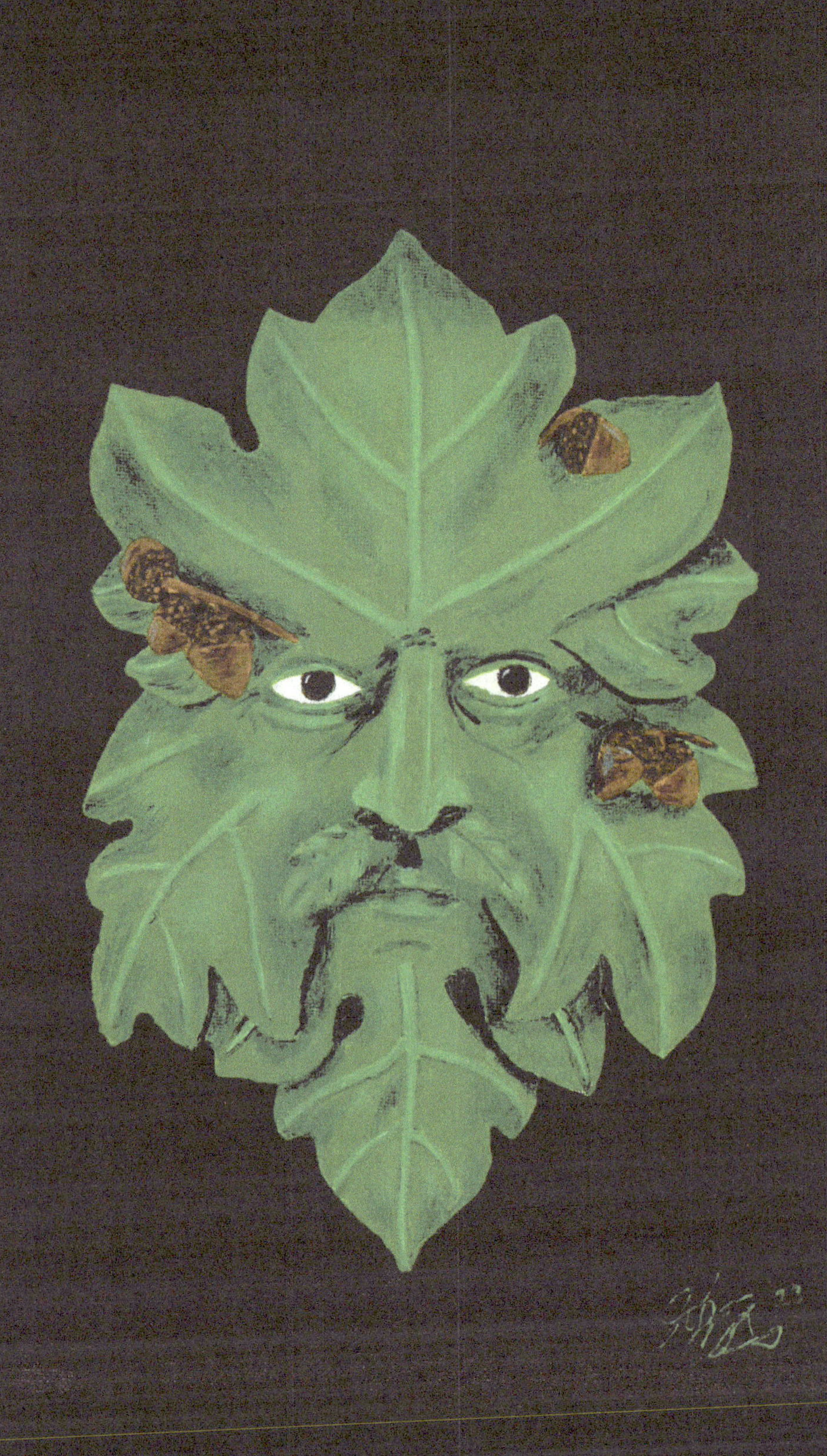

CellCraft: A Prisoner's Guide to Witchcraft
by Eracüs Wolfkrow

Intro:

Wicca AKA The Craft or Witchcraft is all about nature and the balance of female and male energy. Prison, on the other hand is an unnatural place full of imbalance and chaos, mentally, physically and spiritually. Convicts tend to go to extremes.

This book CellCraft is about how we learned to adapt and practice witchcraft without the tools and other items previously thought necessary.

We hope you never find yourself in a situation like prison. But as the world becomes more and more unbalanced may our lessons we've learned in the school of knocks also help you in your journey.

Likewise if you have any comments, questions or suggestions from your experience, you can contact their authors through abocomix.com.

Eracüs WolfKrow

Altar Tool Creation

Well in this school of hard knocks it's not easy getting real altar tools. You see, what is an Athame to us… Well, to the guards they look like weapons. So, you may see the problem we have. Now let's go back in time when us Witches were being killed. They used mundane items to act in for the real thing. So as our forefathers we must do likewise with the things we got in here.

We acquired an illustration board and drew all of our tools and candles, as shown in Figure 1 of this chapter. We as Shaman like to use the same symbols that correspond with each tool.

Figure 1

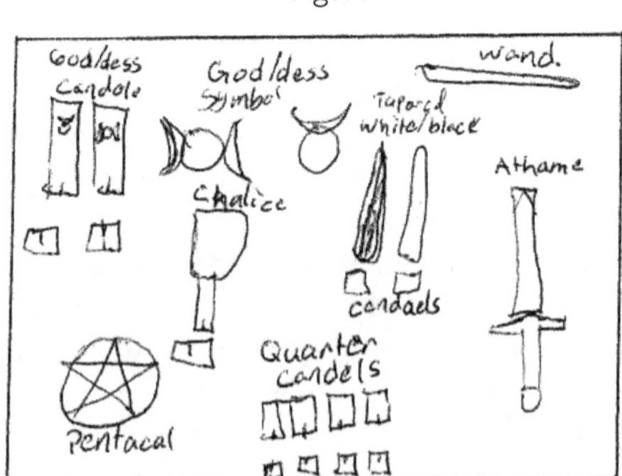

Now as we talk about the altar tools and things we will tell you about them. So, after you draw all of the tools you can color it to match that of the ones that you can have outside of these walls. No, you do not have to draw all of the tools mentioned here. But I will put all of those we know and use.

Tool of the Craft

Altar Cloth

This can be made of any cloth or bought at a Craft store with multiple designs. It is useful to catch wax or ashes so it does not ruin the altar itself. There are some types with magick symbols like the Pentagram, Triple Goddess, etc. but if your unit/policy does not allow it (like where we are) then you can use a handkerchief from commissary. You may draw craft symbols on it. A common one is black in color, but you can use what fits your purpose.

Ashpot
This is a pot to place ash from burning incense, spell paper and spell components. Traditionally the incense is burned at Samhain, or a ritual that suits you. We feel it's better to release it to nature in the wind.

Asperger
This is used to sprinkle holy water or potions to bless and consecrate the circle. You can also use a favorite tree branch if you wish.

Basket
These are used when doing work outdoors or in a big gathering to carry the needed ritual tools and items.

Bell
Ritual bells are usually made of silver, pewter or brass, and can be used to call the quarter and deities.

Besom
A witch's broom is a symbol of purification. It is usually made with ash or birch pole, and broom or birch bristles wrapped in willow. It is used to cleanse the circle space before ritual cleansing our psychic debris.

Boline
This blade is differentiated from the athame because it is used to cut other ritual material. Usually used on ceremonial gathering of herbs, sometimes shaped as a crescent sickle.

Bowl
Vessel used to hold water or oil; it can be another symbol of Water element.

Candles
These are the elemental symbol of Fire and can be used for specific intentions, such as representing or invoking the Goddess and God.

Cauldron
Flame-proof metal container used to burn, brew and mix things. The three support prongs symbolize the triple Goddess and the two points for the handle is the dual God.

Crown
Some traditions use a crown: a silver crescent crown for the priestess and a horned one for the priest.

Crystal Ball
This device of a Witch is used to divine the answers of questions.

Incense
Sacred herbs burned to create a sacred space and add energy to a ritual.

Libation Bowl
For offerings to the Gods in thanks for their help.

Mask
Ceremonial tool used in covens for High Priestess and High Priest.

Mirror
Used for scrying, much like a crystal ball. They can reflect the light of the Moon or Sun onto the priestess or altar tools to empower them.

Book of Shadows
A blank lined book to write out spells or record rituals and other things in the Craft.

Peyton
A ritual pentacle symbolizing the spirit, used to open gateways, evoke the divine, and protect and bless ritual tools and food.

Salt
Sea or Kosher salt is mixed in with water. Other traditions substitute salt with pieces of black coral since both are items of protection.

Scourge
A cat o' nine tails used to induce ritual consciousness by drawing blood from the body and away from the brain.

Scythe/Sickle
A crescent blade to represent the Goddess in Her moon phase.

Staff
Staves are often the height of the practitioner or slightly shorter. If the staff is forked at the top, it is called a Stang, a symbol of the horned God.

Sword
A double-edged blade, much like the athame and wand, used to cast a circle for initiation ceremonies of traditional covens. One is asked by sword point to only enter in Perfect Love and Perfect Trust.

Meditation

With our limited resources it can be hard to meditate. If you need a bowl or a meditation bowl for noise, or if you need a baby waterfall and incense, that is where it's hard.

I've come up with some ways to do so. For the waterfall I always make it to where my sink has water coming out non-stop. Now for the meditation bowl I'll hit my steel stool to cause the vibration sound. Now on the incense I have no way to get it done.

Now I use Mala prayer beads to meditate as a fidget toy, because it's hard to slow my thoughts. I use them as a count, and a mantra style of meditation. When it comes to meditation it is better if you do so alone. Yet if you can't then it is okay.

Get into a meditative position and Visualize a giant screen before you. This is your mind's eye. Visualize the number 12 and go all the way to 1 counting down. Then count backwards from 13 to 1 but do not visualize the number. Now when you do so it will be easier to meditate.

Once in this deep mindset you can go to your sacred place. As for me I'm in a snow caped wooded Mountain. As I walk up to a Willow I try to see an opening. I walk into it and inside is like a cave with a Thron and symbols of Morrighan (my Goddess) and Dagda (my God). Also, my familiars and spirit animals are there.

Now count forward from 1 to 13 and again 1 to 12. After this wiggle your toes and hands to get circulation back.

Degree System

In Witchcraft or Neo Pagan there is a Degree System. In the Craft (no
not the movie 👋) you will come across Five degree systems. The first is
more a more traditional 3-degree system in which you start as a Neophyte.
Then when you have done or gone through a year-in-a-day study of the
Craft, on the last day you will do a 1st degree initiation ritual. If you're in a
coven then it will be done with you by a priestess if you're male, and a priest
if a female. Yet if you are a solitary practitioner of course it will be done alone
with the God or Goddess.

Now if you want to have a Craft name this is a time to pick one. To pick
their names many Craft members use different methods from Numerology.
Some also go by names from Mythology or Fantasy books. Yet I've also seen a
Magus' Mentor or Teacher give the initiate their Craft name.

I will discuss more on Craft names in a different time. Back to degrees:
the year-and-a-day will start again until the final degree is done, and you
are 3rd degree Witch/Magus. The figure below shows the Traditional Degree Symbols. A basic understanding of history, ethics, mythology, theology
and holiday are required to know to be a first degree. As well as meditation,
Psychic, and Energy work skills, starting a Magick journal, ritual participating,
training in the art of healing, setting up a personal altar, learning to cleanse,
bless and protect the home and circle. The most important thing in all is to
know The Wiccan Rede as a day-to-day reality.

The second degree you will be considered a Priest or Priestess. You will
be able to lead a ritual, cast a magick circle, and do spells. The third-degree
of traditional Witchcraft is a honoring as High Priest/ess in which you are in
Cosmic Union with the divine.

Traditional Degree Symbols

First Degree   Second Degree   Third Degree

Now most of your Ceremonial Craft skools (I know it's spelled school,
just except my madness) use ten initiation degrees based off of the Qaba-
listic Tree of Life. Other skools of the Craft use a seven-degree system off
of the seven Chakras or the Seven Magickal Planets. The symbols for the
Magickal Planets use the planetary symbols. Some use the Twelve Signs of
the Zodiac. Skools like Penczak's Temple Tradition uses the five-degree system of the Five Elements of Life.

What Degree system you use is entirely up to you and the skool you choose. This is your path: it ends and begins with you, only to end again, and begin again.

Wiccan Rede[*]

Bide the Wiccan laws ye must, in Perfect Love and Perfect Trust.
Live and let live, fairly take and fairly give.
Cast the Circle Thrice about to keep the Evil Spirits out.
To bind the Spell every time, Let the spell be spake in rhyme.
Soft of eye and light of touch, Speak little, listen much.
Deosil go by the Waxing Moon, sing and dance the Wiccan Rune.
Widder shins go when the moon doth wane, and the werewolf howls by the dread Wolfsbane.
When the Lady's Moon is new, Kiss thy hand to Her times two.
When the Moon rides at Her Peak then your hearts desire seek.
Heed the North winds mighty gale; lock the door and drop the sail.
When the Wind comes from the South, Love will Kiss thee, on the mouth.
When the wind blows from the East, expect the new and set the feast.
When the west wind blows o'er thee, departed spirits restless be.
Nine woods in the Cauldron go, burn them quick a' burn them slow.
Elder be ye Lady's tree burn it not or cursed ye'll be.
When the Wheel begins to turn, let the Beltane fires burn.
When the Wheel has turned at Yule, light the log and let Pan rule.
Heed ye flower, bush and tree, by the Lady Bless'd Be.
Where the rippling waters go cast a stone and truth ye'll know.
When find that ye have need, hearken not to other's greed.
With the fool no season spend or be counted as his friend.
Merry meet and merry part, bright the cheeks and warm the heart.
Mind the Threefold Law ye must three times bad and three times good.
When misfortune is enow, Wear the Blue star on thy brow.
True in love ever be unless thy lover's false to thee.
Eight words ye Wiccan Rede be, An' it harm none, do as ye will.

[*] This is the author's adaptation of the "The Rede of the Wiccae," written by Lady Gwen Thompson and attributed to her grandmother, Adriana Porter. It was first published in *Green Egg* magazine, no. 69 (Ostara 1975).

The Living Goddess

The Goddess of All,
    supreme and divine.
Our Great Mother Earth,
    the Cosmic Sunshine.
The Goddess of Life,
    the Mistress of Death.
She gives us birth,
    She is our breath.
The Goddess of Love,
    the Mistress of Hate.
She spins our thread
    and weaves our Fate.
The Goddess within us,
    the Goddess without;
Rid us of troubles,
    remove all our doubt.
The Living Goddess incarnate,
    i bow to Her feet;
i worship Her image
    in each Woman I meet!

- jennifer amelia rose

Witches' Creed*

Hear now the words of the Witches,
the secrets we hid in the night,
When dark was our destiny's Path
that now we bring forth into light.

Mysterious Water and fire,
the earth and the wide-ranging air,
by hidden quintessence we know them,
and will and keep silent and dare.

The birth and rebirth of all nature,
the passing of winter and spring,
we share with the life Universal,
rejoice in the magickal ring.

Four times in the year the Great Sabbat
returns, and the witches are seen
at Lammas and Candlemas dancing,
on May Eve and old Halloween.

When day-time and night-time are equal,
When sun is at its greatest and least,
the four Lesser Sabbats are Summoned,
and again gather Witches in feast.

Thirteen Silver moons in a year
Thirteen is the Coven's array
Thirteen times at Esbat make merry,
for each golden year-and-a-day.

The Power was passed down the ages
each time between woman and man
each century unto the other,
ere times and the ages began.

When drawn is the magickal Circle,
by sword or athame of power,
its compass between the two worlds lies
in land of the shades for that hour.

This world has no right then to know it.
and world of beyond will tell naught.

The oldest of Gods are invoked there,
the Great Work of magic is wrought.

For two are the mystical pillars
that stand at the gate of the shrine,
and two are the powers of nature,
the forms and the forces divine

The dark and the light in succession
the opposites each unto each
Shown forth as a God and a Goddess;
of this did our ancestors teach.

By night He's the wild wind's rider,
the Horned One, the Lord of the Shades.
By day He's the King of the Woodland,
the dweller in green of forest glades.

She is youthful or Old as She pleases,
She sails the torn Cloud in Her barque,
the bright Silver lady of midnight,
the Crone who weaves spells in the dark.

The Master and Mistress of Magick
they dwell in the deeps of the mind
immortal and ever-renewing,
with power to free or to bind.

So drink the good wine to the Old Gods
and dance and make love in their praise,
'till Elphames fair land shall receive us
In the Peace at the end of our days.

And do what you will be the Challenge,
So be it in love that harms none,
for this is the only commandment.
By Magick of old it be done!

Eight words the Witches' Creed fulfill
If it harms none, thy will be done!

* This is the author's adaptation of Doreen Valiente, "The Witches' Creed," in *Witchcraft for Tomorrow* (London: Hale, 1978), pp. 172–173.

The Witches' Rune*

Darksome night and Shining Moon
East then South then West then North
Harken to the Witches Rune
Here we come to call thee forth

Earth and Water, air and fire
Wand and Pentacle and Sword
Work ye into our desire
And come ye as the Charm is made.

Queen of Heaven, Queen of Hell
Horned Hunter of the Night
Lend your Power ye unto life
And work our will by magick rite.

By all the powers of the land and sea
By all the might of the Moon and Sun
As we do will, so mote it be
Chant the spell and be it done.

EKO, EKO Raziel
EKO, EKO Azrael
EKO, EKO Neit
EKO, EKO Morrighan

Chant

We are the Earth
We are the Green
We are the Love
We are the Dream

* This is the author's adaptation of Doreen Valiente , "The Witches' Rune" originally written for the *Gardnerian Book of Shadows* (ca. 1953) and later published in *The Witches' Way* (1981, London: Hale).

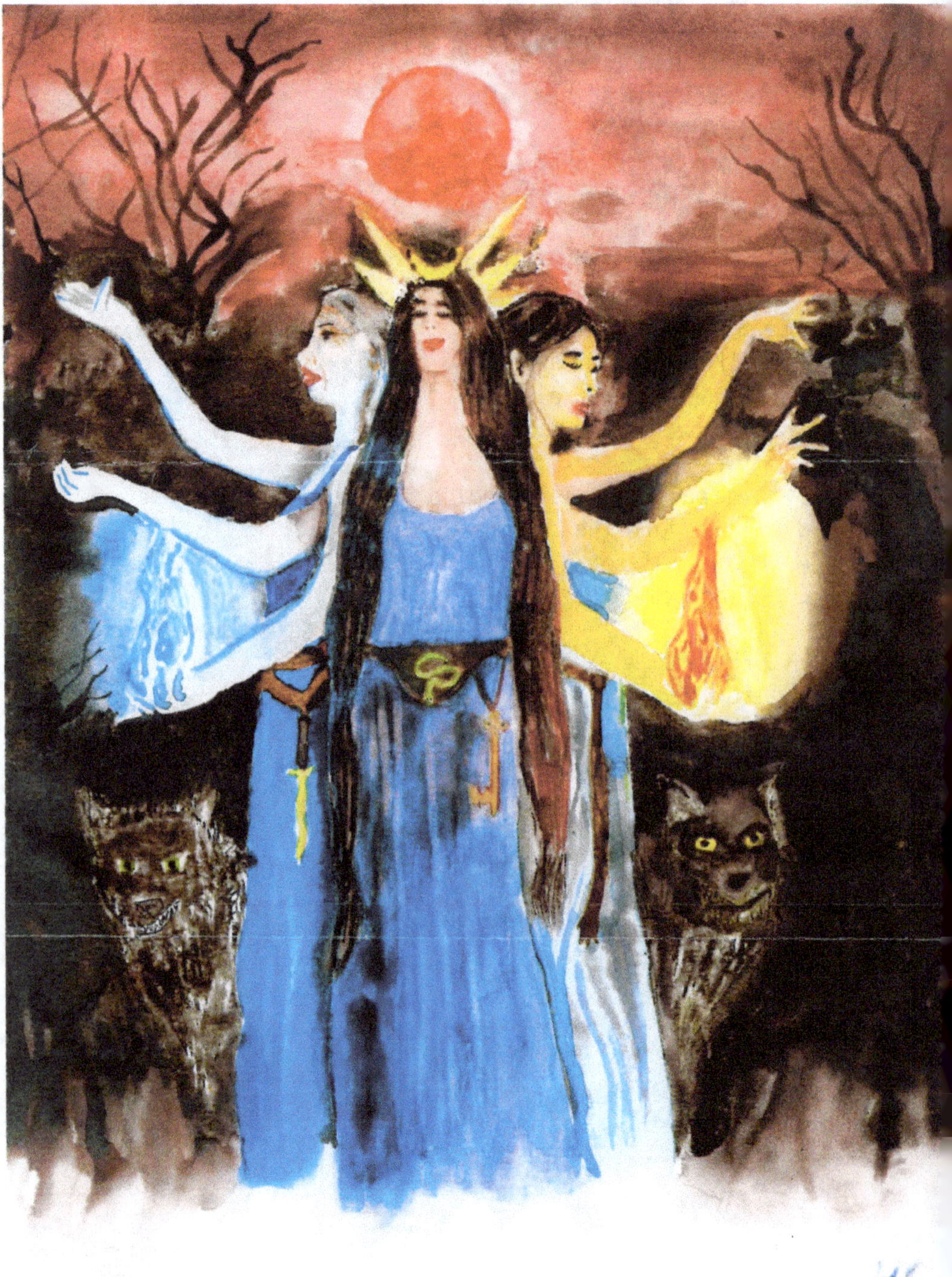

Wicca in Prison
by Gary Farlow

The standard misconception about Wicca in prison is based in ignorance and fear. Those who are practitioners of Wicca are thought to be "devil worshippers," and when one informs these ill-informed individuals that Wicca doesn't even believe in a "Satan" or "hell," it is met with disbelief.

Equally disparaging are the views that Wicca is a refuge for orgies and merely a hangout or place to "hook up" for a sexual encounter. Again, a myth.

I grew up in a Christian home, the youngest of eight and a child of the 1960's civil rights era. The fiery oratory and social movements for racial justice and gender equality typically overlooked gays.

Being a gay youth in the South of that time meant "hiding in plain sight." It simply wasn't discussed. The established views and dogma of mainstream Christianity left me feeling, as Mel White wrote, "A Stranger At The Gate."

Once I entered prison, in an ironic twist, I found a certain freedom. I was at liberty to explore other faiths, I seek a "home" for my spiritual journey.

In the prison chapel I discovered an entire library of Wiccan books. In prison one is usually at liberty to attend any religious service held, so I began to explore the Wiccan faith.

Initially, I found the group accepting and tolerant. There were other gays, but equally there were straight, Trans, and as well others who were declared Christians, Humanists, even a Buddhist and Asatru.

Formal instruction using material from (now defunct) Millennial Kingdom School of Witchcraft. Two years of applied study led me to achieve level 1 Witch. Utilizing the book "365 And A Day" I pursued my studies with zeal and developed my own Book of Shadows.

Our group was now led by an inmate who claimed to be a Level 3 High Priest of Alexandrian Wicca. What had been a congenial group epitomized by acceptance and tolerance became meetings in which all other faiths were criticized and treated with contempt — not a Wiccan practice.

Slowly the group shrank. By ones and twos individuals ceased attending Wiccan services or studies. Where once over 30 frequently gathered, now a scant 3 or 4 were now there.

Ultimately, I, too left. Leaving me with a bad taste much as did mainstream Christianity and even the Metropolitan Community Church (the "gay" denomination), I discovered the Unitarian Universalist Church of the Larger Fellowship. In it I could "window shop" and blend in aspects of Wicca, Christianity, Buddhism, even Islam and Humanism to chart my own unique spiritual path.

I no longer identify as "Wiccan" as I have an utter dislike of "labels" that restrict one's freedom to believe or find solace in the charity of Islam, the compassion of Buddhism, the peace of Christianity and the mysticism of Wicca. I continue on my own unique journey of self-discovery, no longer boxed-in by branding as "this" or "that" but free to explore, try, adopt and "be" — simply me.

I composed a lot of poetry to celebrate the Wiccan year, I've attached two of these.

Litha

Walk with me,
    talk with me,
    tell me your heart's desire.
Speak to me,
    commune with me,
    as we lay beside a midsummer's fire.
Litha is here,
    and summer is nigh,
    as days reach a zenith 'neath the sun.
So come with me,
    take my hand,
    for you my love are my only one.

'Tis Mabon

After the close of Summer
    before the land lies 'neath snow,
    there comes the Magic of Autumn
    when all nature is aglow
Days grow ever shorter,
    harvest time is nigh,
    'tis Mabon now my love,
    as Mother Earth breathes a sigh.
The Moon shines in her glory,
    reflecting Maiden, Mother, Crone,
    the Wiccan Year comes full circle,
    like our love which we show.
So arise my one and come away,
    let us sing, feast and make love,
    for Wiccan Mabon is a celebration,
    of the Goddess' bounty from above.

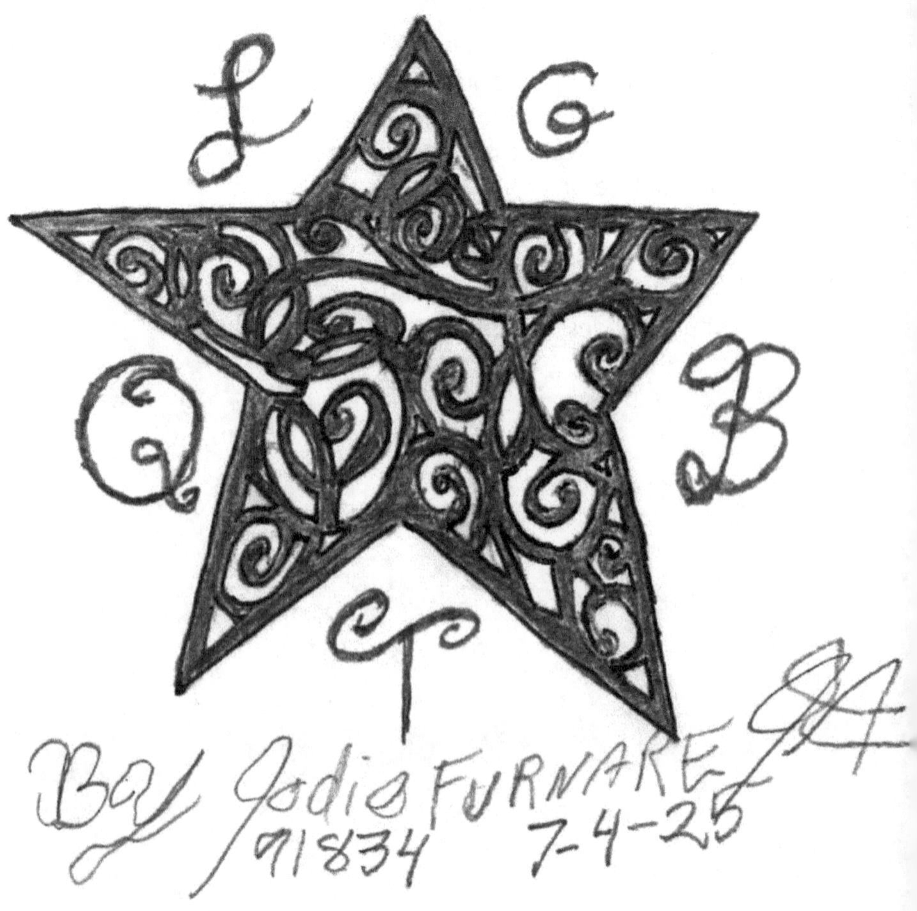
L G
Q B
By JodieFurnare
91834   7-4-25

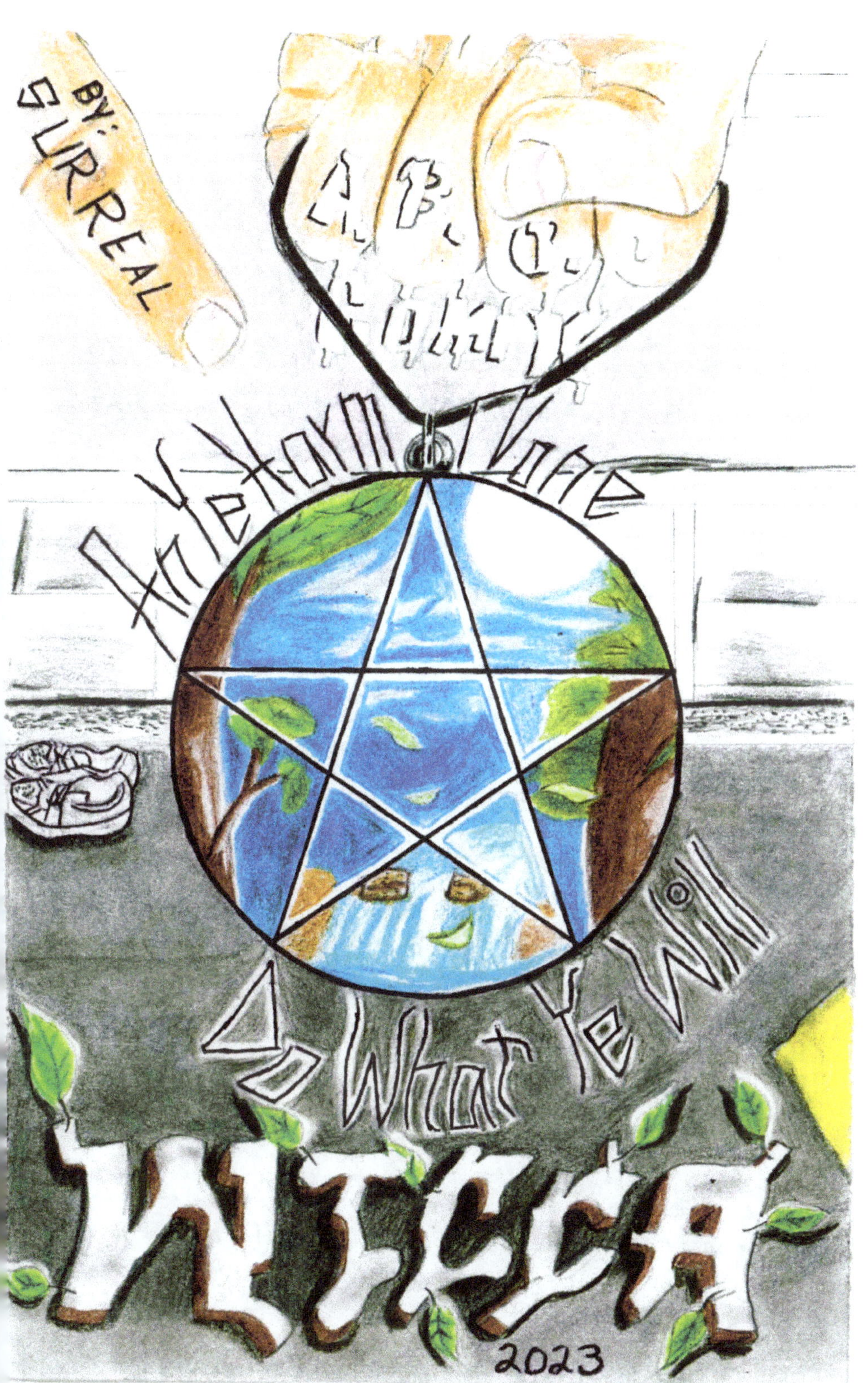
BY: SURREAL
WITCH
2023

MY EXPERIENCES IN WICCA. Blessed be.

I'm still a beginner. There's still much to learn. I know about the tools and the reasons why each tool is used. I know how to cast circles and how to close them. I never do nothing unless I know what I'm doing. That's why it's best to find someone who can teach you the ways of it. Also remember the gods and the goddesses will choose you. You may find or read one that's just like you but just watch for the signs. I have a picture that in the winkles of the shirt revealed Zeus "♃". My favorite color is purple. Which Zeus's color is purple. Note: Your brothers and sisters is the rocks, the water anything nature without these fancy buildings. Most Wicca "beginner" books have the same info but you have to read to find the author thats easy for you to understand. It's like drawing. There are so many to choose from so its best to read each one. For spells, you need to do your homework before attempting Magick And have confidence in yourself saying I will succeed.

Movies such as The Craft, which is my favorite movie, as it can show you about witchcraft and the meaning of, "An Ye Harm none, Do What Ye Will".

Note: "Blessed be" is a old language that witches back then greet one of another. Can also be said as goodbye.

Tools used in Wicca.
~This is all from memory~

The Wand	Used	Reason?
Anything wood or wood-like "tree nut"	To speak with spirits. You can't see them but feel its presence	Spirits are like friends and a wand wont scare them away Your be helped.

The Sword	Used	Reason
	To cast (draw) a larger circle	The bigger the diameter like a football field, the sword will cover.

The Knife or Boline is a black handle dagger-like blade thats dull as a butter knife.	Used	Reason
	This is your cutting tool only It's not a weapon	This is when after casting a circle that one of you or your members needs to exit or vice versa come in.

The broom is really a show item. Other than sweeping your area free from any dirt, it can be useful when consecrating. To consecrate means to make it pure, honorable for the gods & goddesses watching over us.

You cut like a slice of cake by raising it infront of you and moving it to the right then moving it to the left to close the circle once they're in.

The Meaning Behind the Practices of Wicca.

Without the circle is called a Pentacle.

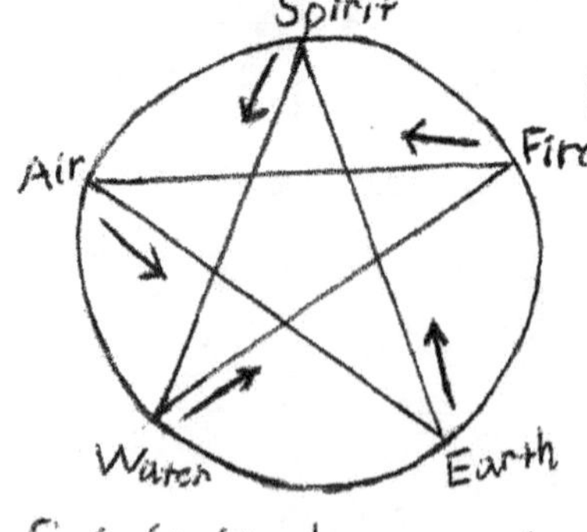

Spirit is always pointed up.
If Spirit is pointed down, then you're letting anything in your circle.

There are 5 elements used:

Fire, Water Earth, Air & Spirit.

The pentagram represents:

Man or it could be Woman, but I was told "Man."

The circle is a sphere.

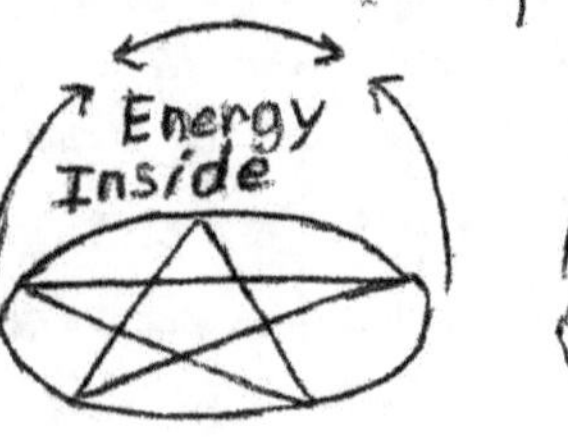

Easy way to remember

The sphere of energy protects you from inside. A circle is endless. There's no angles. Thats why a circle is used.

Next page I'll tell you how to cast circles.

When casting a circle, here is a useful tip to determine where East is as witches face East. Sun raises on the East. Sets on the West. Now follow this diagram if walking in your cell, if you lay toward the left hand

Standing in the center, Face East and hold out your hand (doesn't matter which hand). Now with your index finger pointing, close your eyes and visualize at the tip of your finger a blue flame. Now open your eyes and start drawing, starting East, turning slowly South, turning West, turning North, then turning back to East. Congratulations, you just cast your circle. To close your circle, make sure to cover everything you did, Then retrace going Counter Clockwise East → North → West → South → East and thanking them.

If your performing a spell or a ritual which anytime your doing something like writing a paper taking step-by-step then it's called a ritual. Everybody does rituals if you think about it.

You will need protection so when facing East say, "I call for the Guardians of the East Watch Towers, speaking it outloud and telling them "please protect this circle."

Facing South, say, "I call for the Guardians of the <u>South</u> Watch Towers", adding, "please remove any negativity that's inside this circle."

Facing West, say, "I call for the Guardians of the <u>West</u> Watch Towers, adding, "please keep my mind focus and thinking my purpose only."

Facing North, say, "I call for the Guardians of the <u>North</u> Watch Towers", adding, "please remove any evil that may be here". Now Face East.

Follow the guildlines above when calling for extra protection from your gods & goddesses.

You can read what I wrote but its highly recommended to speak from your heart.

It's a more beautiful relationship when they hear from you then reading out of a book

Priestess of Cybele

O Goddess Cybele!
    Please hear my Cry!
To be One with Your Spirit,
    i'm willing to die!
O Great Mother Earth,
    to You i belong, so strong;
i am your Daughter forever,
    the Son is now gone!
O Mother Nature,
    Please show me the Way.
You give Light in the Darkness,
    and resurrect Life each day.
A Priestess of Cybele,
    which i've become in position,
One of the Gallae i lay prostrate,
    A sacred rite—sexual transition!
O Divine Feminine image,
    i worship at your feet.
i offer my Self with kisses,
    to live as a Woman discreet.
Beautiful as the violets
    and bright as the Full Moon,
i'll sing your praises with devotion Love,
    Forever i'll rest in Your Bosom soon!

- jennifer amelia rose

from: The Ultimate Book of Shadows
(for the New Generation) Solitary Witch By SilverRaven Wolf

Pagan Pride

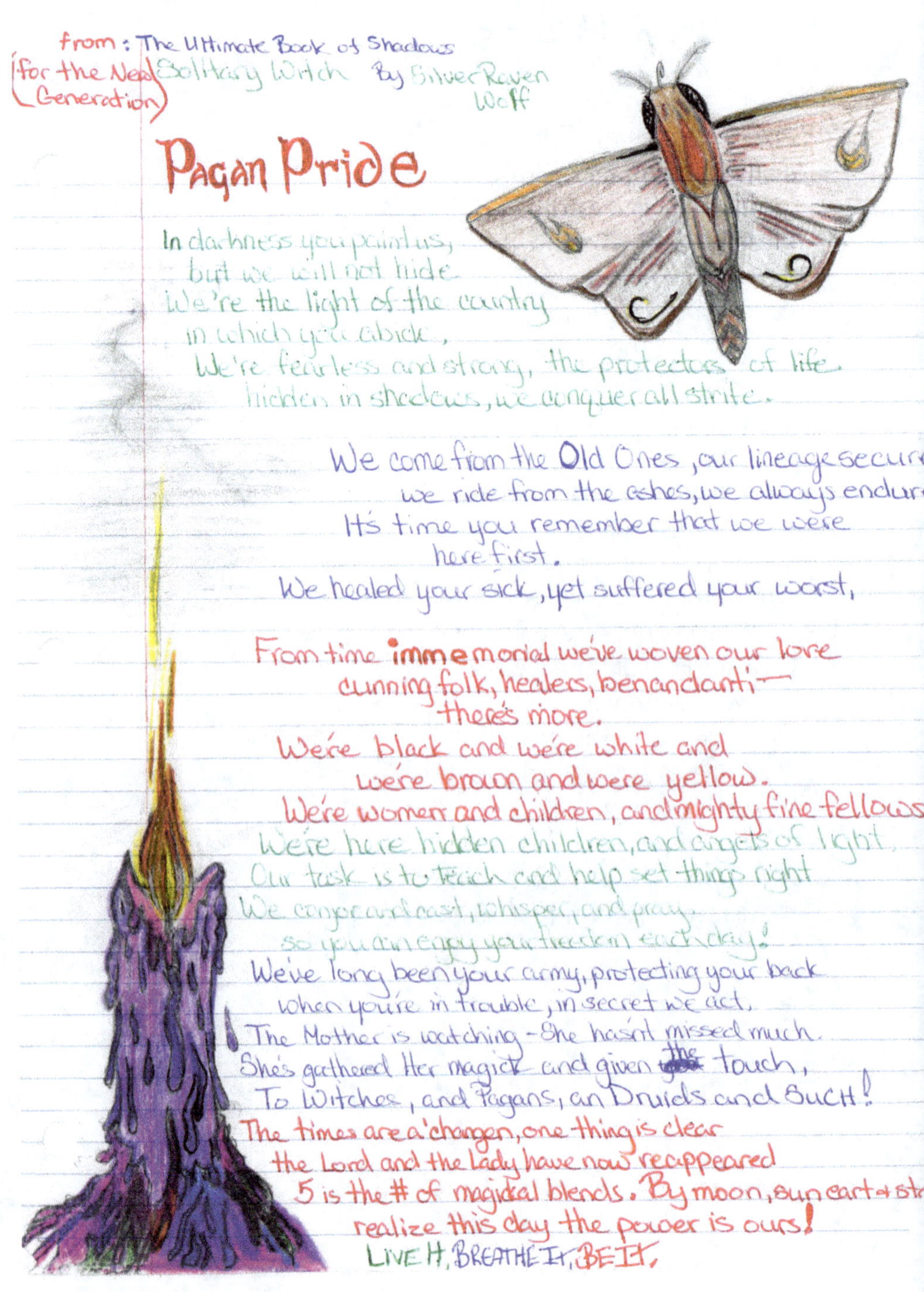

In darkness you paint us,
    but we will not hide.
We're the light of the country
    in which you abide,
    We're fearless and strong, the protectors of life,
    hidden in shadows, we conquer all strife.

We come from the Old Ones, our lineage secure
        we rise from the ashes, we always endure
    It's time you remember that we were
            here first.
We healed your sick, yet suffered your worst,

From time **imm**emorial we've woven our lore
        cunning folk, healers, benandanti—
            there's more.
We're black and we're white and
        we're brown and we're yellow.
    We're women and children, and mighty fine fellows
We're here hidden children, and angels of light,
Our task is to teach and help set things right
We conjure and cast, whisper, and pray,
    so you can enjoy your freedom each day!
We've long been your army, protecting your back
    when you're in trouble, in secret we act.
The Mother is watching – She hasn't missed much.
She's gathered Her magick and given the touch,
To Witches, and Pagans, an Druids and SUCH!
The times are a'changen, one thing is clear
the Lord and the Lady have now reappeared
5 is the # of magickal blends. By moon, sun earth + star
realize this day the power is ours!
LIVE IT, BREATHE IT, BE IT.

Circle in a Cage
by Tammy Jean Norman
aka Phoenix-Electra

In 2016, I was placed in San Bernardino county awaiting trial. In the three and a half years I was there I faced many, many challenges. Not only was I persecuted for being a Trans-Woman in an all-male facility, I was also pushed about because I was a Witch. I managed to gather up three other like-minded people in Jail who would help me practice. The C/Os would not allow us out for services at the same time since I was on the top tier, and they were on the bottom tier.

Well, we hatched a plan. During their dayroom time, we cast a circle, one side in the cage I was in, and the other side was outside the cage in the dayroom. We had done this twice before a C/O noticed and angrily tried to break us up. Once that chaplain became involved, he learned about my experience since October 1999. He said "Wow," I've never met a real Witch and from then on, we were all allowed to practice in the dayroom together. With help of the chaplain, we pushed back against haters, and got to practice our faith openly.

It's hard to be a Witch/Pagan in prison since there are almost no organizations to support us like with other faiths. When we have to fight against ignorance, we usually must do it all alone. From getting our religious books and items to just having a space to practice. Without at least 10 or more people, we are often not allowed to practice together. My only wish is that there were more organizations to help support Wiccans in prison so that we don't have to fight with unwilling, power-tripping staff.

A Poem:

Alone, in a dark cell again
Maintaining my faith around such hate
Accused of living my life in sin
I call to my gods and I'm forced to wait
I wish to express my faith as well
Blocked by those who don't understand
While in prayer, I'm Cursed to hell
discrimination still on this "Free Land"
If you wish to know, I'm happy to tell
Open minded one must be
Understanding is easy as well
Just open your eyes to clearly see
I'm no demon, no evil worshiped here
Love for Mother Earth, Ancestors of all
Nothing about me one needs to fear
In our Circle, group so small
We look to help, cure, and love
Taking care of air, land and sea
Casting love spells on the back of a dove
Give love to us, and blessed you'll be
Our laws all summed up into one
All our work times three is done
We do as we will, as love as we harm none
Our Gods are fair with love for everyone

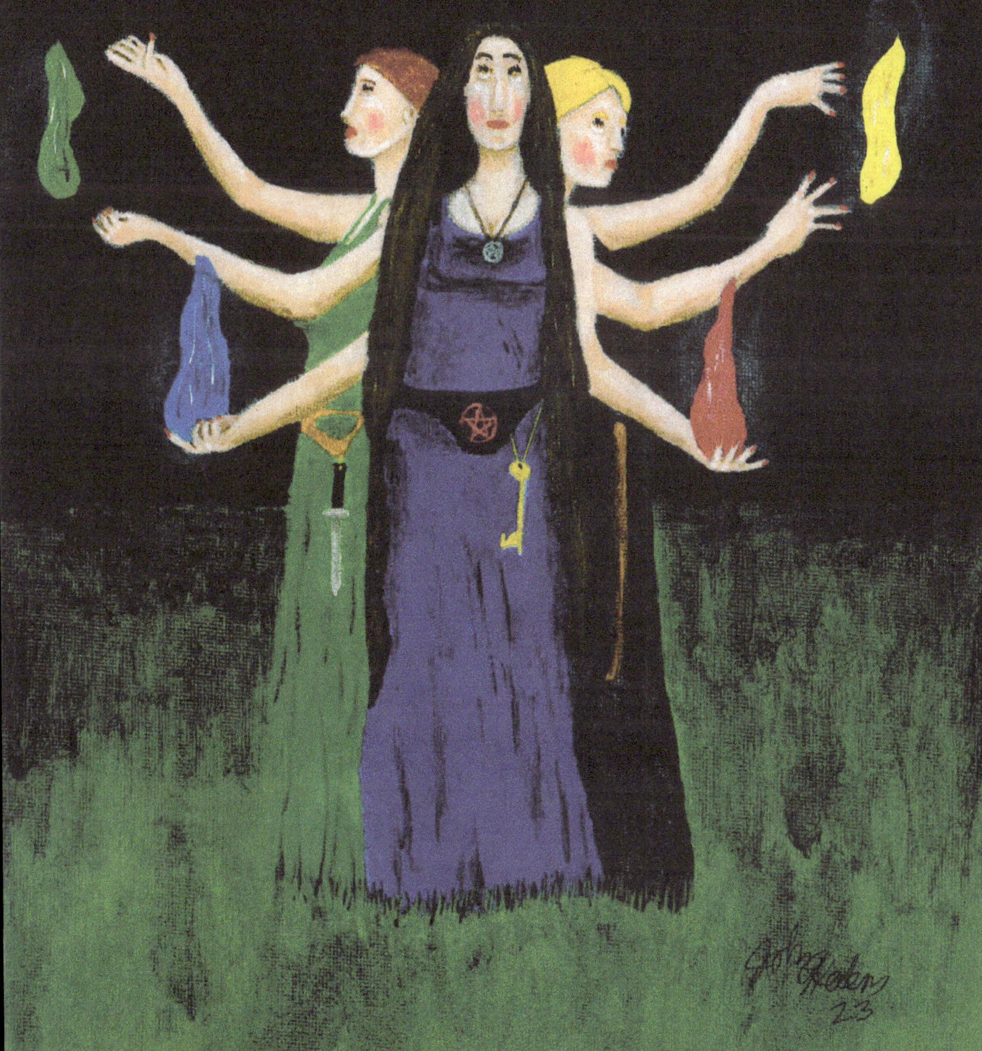

NEW Pagan Service!
by Dottie Cornyx

The catch all service for any of the Non Abrahamic Faiths you may claim, Whether it's Wiccan, Buddhist, actual Neo Pagan, or simply an Agnostic seeker. This is our 2 hrs a week to come together, in an Eclectic Fellowship, teaching in the most general way possible, so as to be as inclusive as possible, and even this was, and remains, a challenge. After a Chaplain change on our unit, we had to change our travel card to Neo Pagan (nothing else will get you a lay in). Unfortunately, this means some of our Non Pagan supporters can no longer join us (a Jewish and a Catholic friend who helped us fill the numbers we first needed).

I had to laugh when I learned that if you filled in Other under Religion (I dislike being labled as anything) they put you down as Christian, nondenominational... It took over a month with several I-60s a week before me and a friend fell out to catch the new Chaplain in his office. Said friend had to go the extra mile to convince the Chaplain he was serious about Pagan service. Apparently being Black means you cannot be spiritually open...

Even now that this is mostly settled, it is still a struggle. Any event that requires the gym, it is our service that is first cut.

Still, I look forward to our time together. Even beyond reconnecting with my spiritual side (something very important in here), I have made some very close friends. We can get together and vent. In a (reasonably) safe space, we get away from the drama on our wings (even if briefly), and it is also a chance to talk our geek hobbies, which most of us share.

And that is "Wicca" at Wallace Unit, TDCJ.

Considering this state, and how far we are from Huntsville, I'm sure it could be worse...

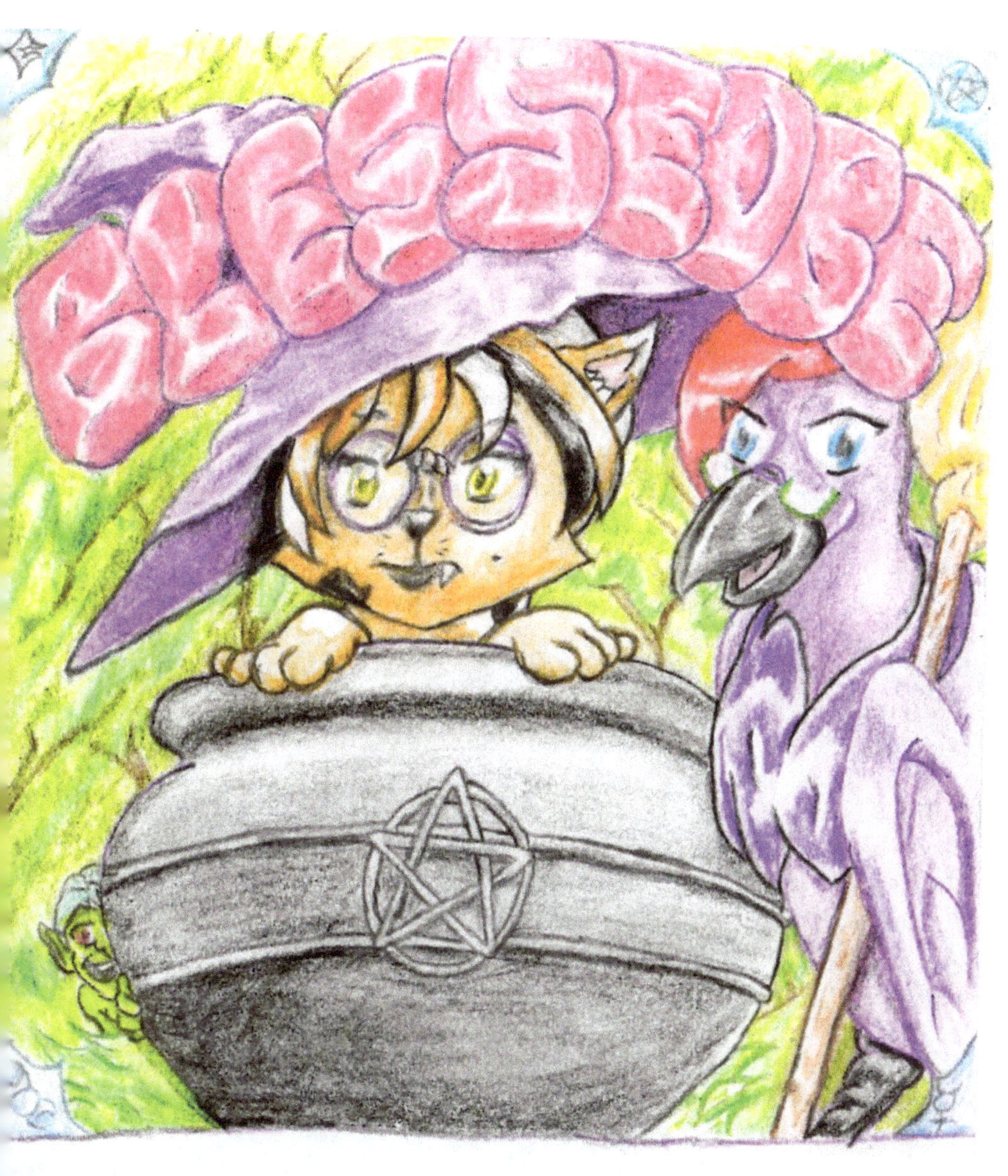
BLESSED BE

The Beauty of Wicca
by Harlequin

Merry Meet! I wanted to write about the beauty of Wicca and the power of the imagination. We all know that prison makes it difficult and sometimes near impossible to practice our Craft. We are extremly limited in what items we can have. Most tools are forbidden, and in some facilities an altar is considered contraband. And then there are the misinformed staff (and other prisoners for that matter) who hold a stigma toward anything remotely pagan. Chaplaincy staff are rarely inclined to accommodate Wiccans, even though Wicca is a recognized religion which is protected by Federal law. Whatever the case may be, there are definite barriers to practice. But the beauty of Wicca is that one doesn't really need tools or even an altar to practice our Craft. In reality, all we truly need is our IMAGINATION. Connecting with Diety is the most important part. Diety is in and within EVERYTHING! So instead of worrying about not having the right materials or being stressed out over the restrictions the prison has over what you can and can not have, remember, rituals can be done entirely in the mind. Calling the Quarters can be done using your finger, and in your mind's eye, imagine candles being lit and elements being invited to join your circle. The Spirits don't care about material things or exact ritual procedures. They only care that you show up and that you enter in perfect peace and with good intentions.

Do yourself a favor, and dont miss out on communicating with Diety. Dont be afraid to dance the sacred mysteries. Spirit is waiting and calling.

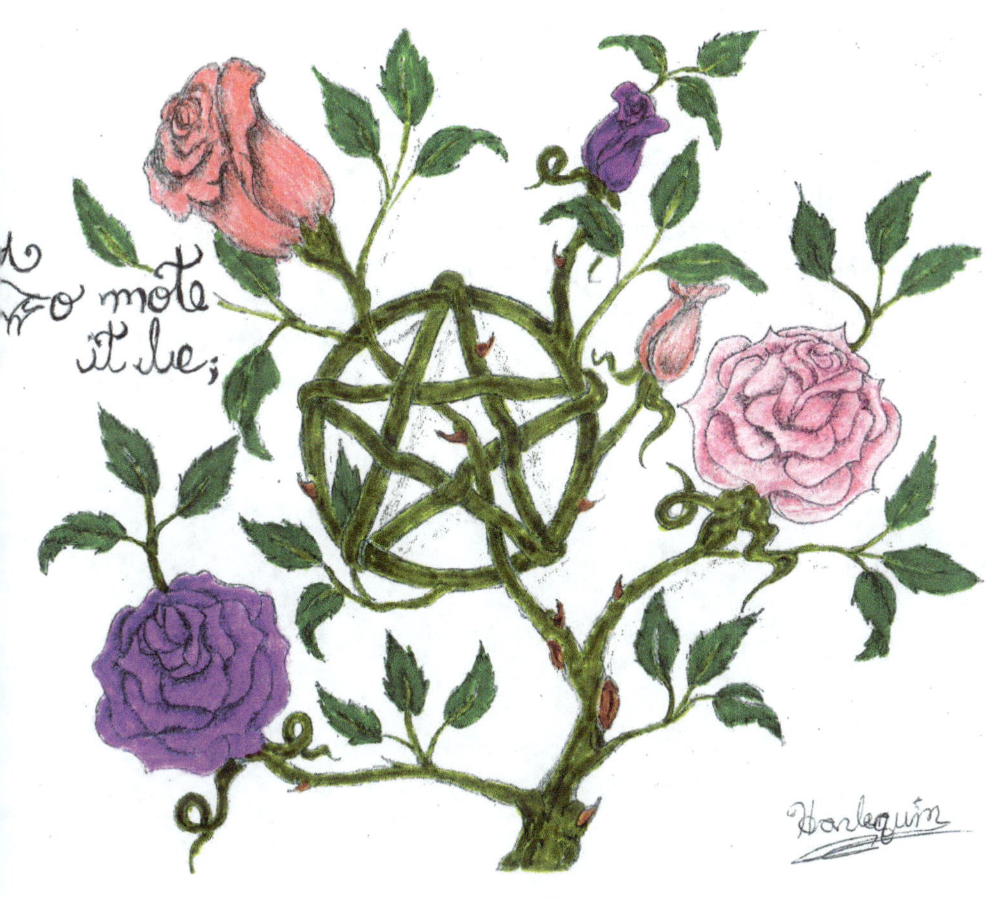

So mote it be;
Harlequin

{Dance of Faith}

Our inner circle is tight knit,
there will be no infiltration.
As the wiccan foretells prophesies
through the moon and constellations.
In meditation...
     We call upon the powers
and through prayer we all listen.
So the lady of wisdom can show you
life's most important mission.
Listen to the song of the world,
stay in time with nature and it's essence.
There is no Satan, only Gods and Goddesses.
You'll find in our presence...

- Charlie Harbert

Don't Cry Little Witch
by The Villain Blvme

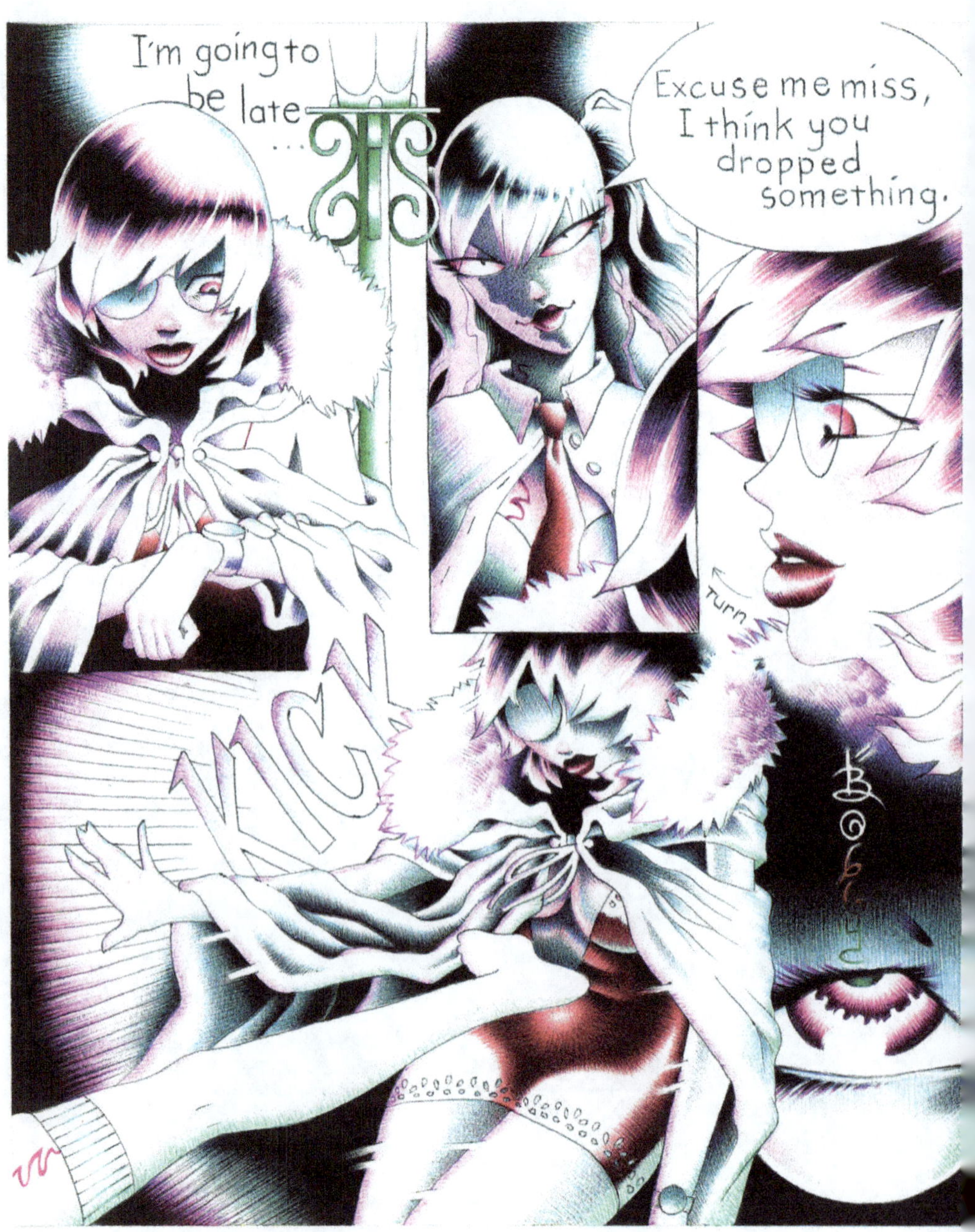
I'm going to
be late ...
Excuse me miss,
I think you
dropped
something.
Turn
KICK

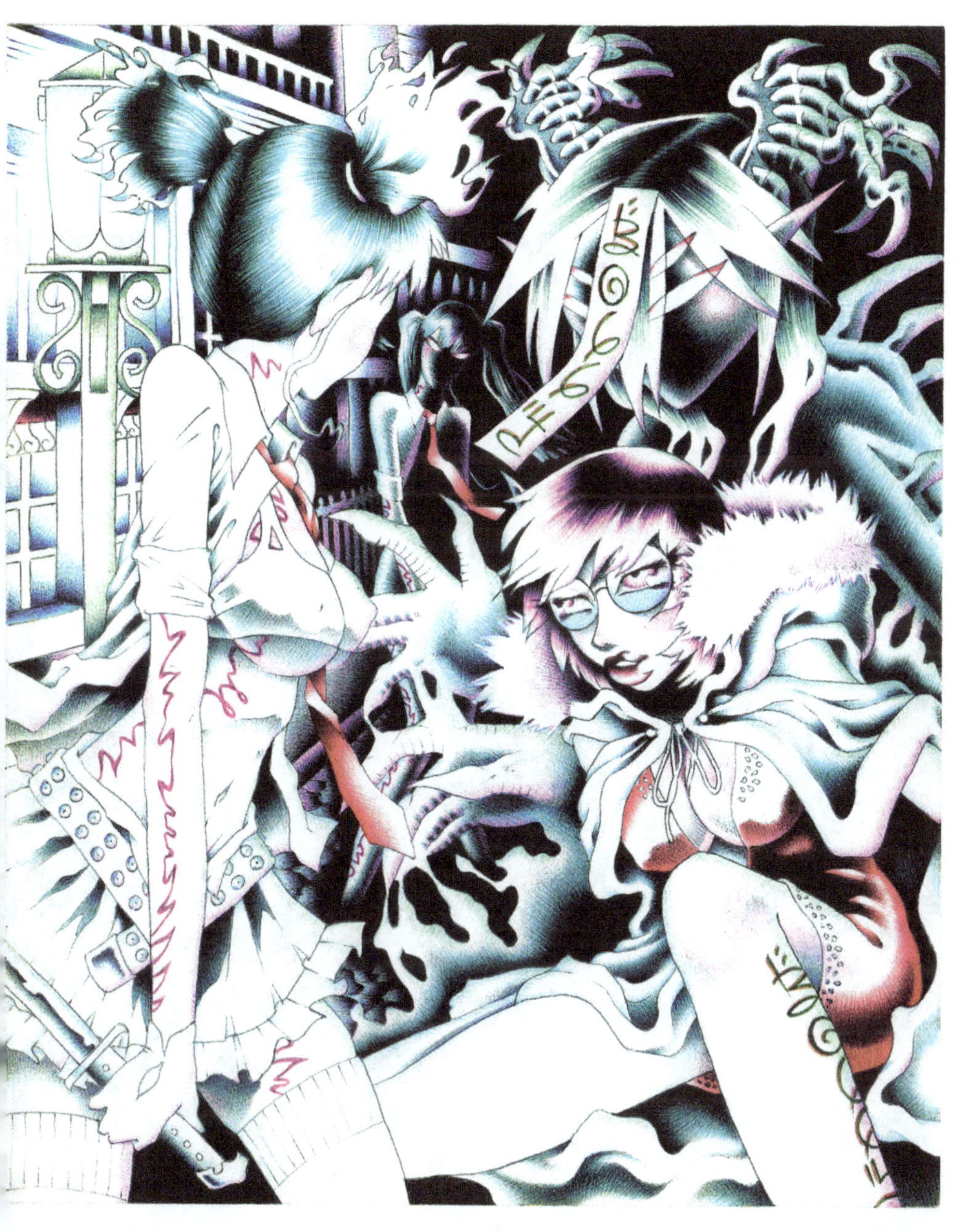

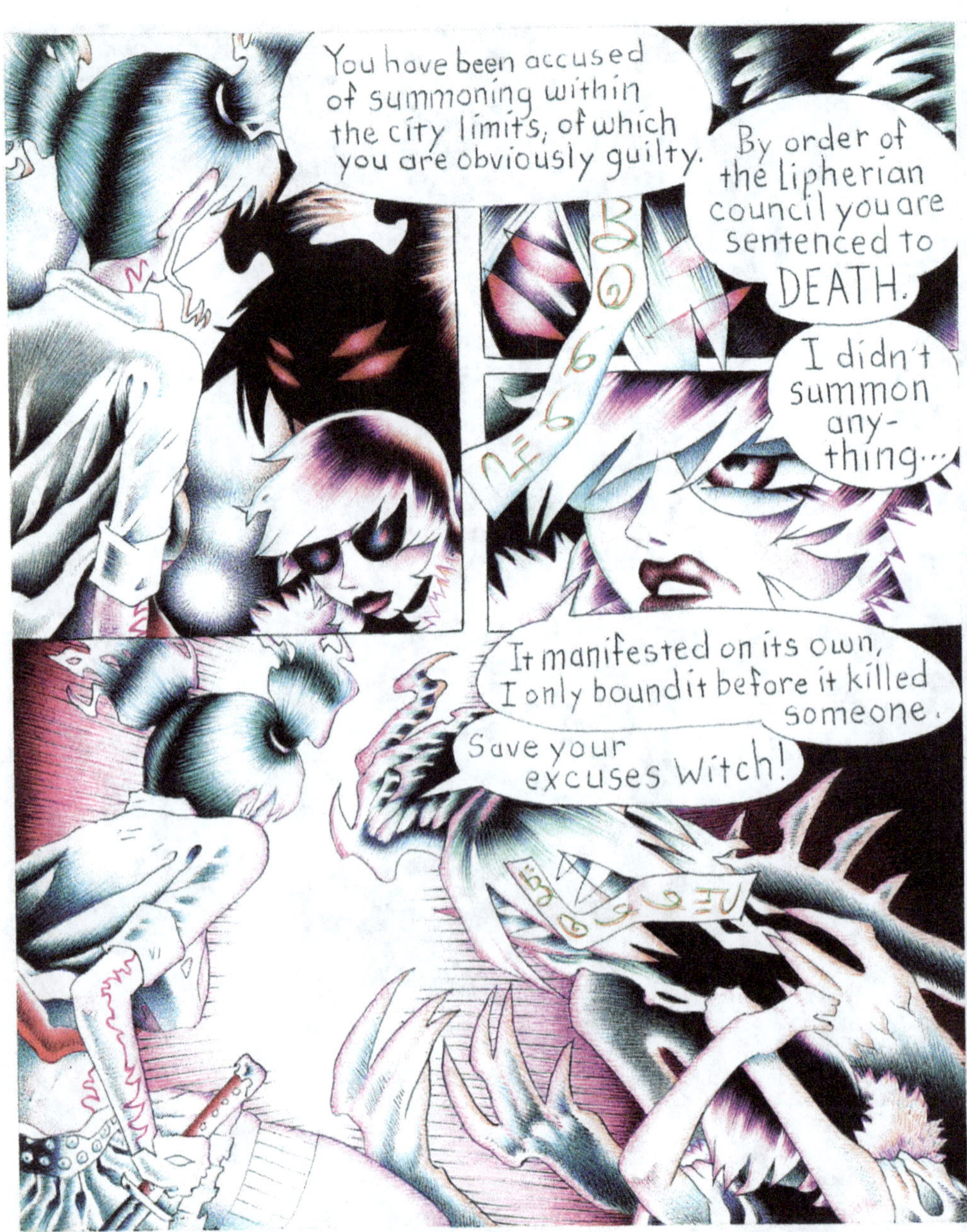

You have been accused of summoning within the city limits, of which you are obviously guilty.
By order of the lipherian council you are sentenced to DEATH.
I didn't summon any- thing...
It manifested on its own, I only bound it before it killed someone.
Save your excuses Witch!

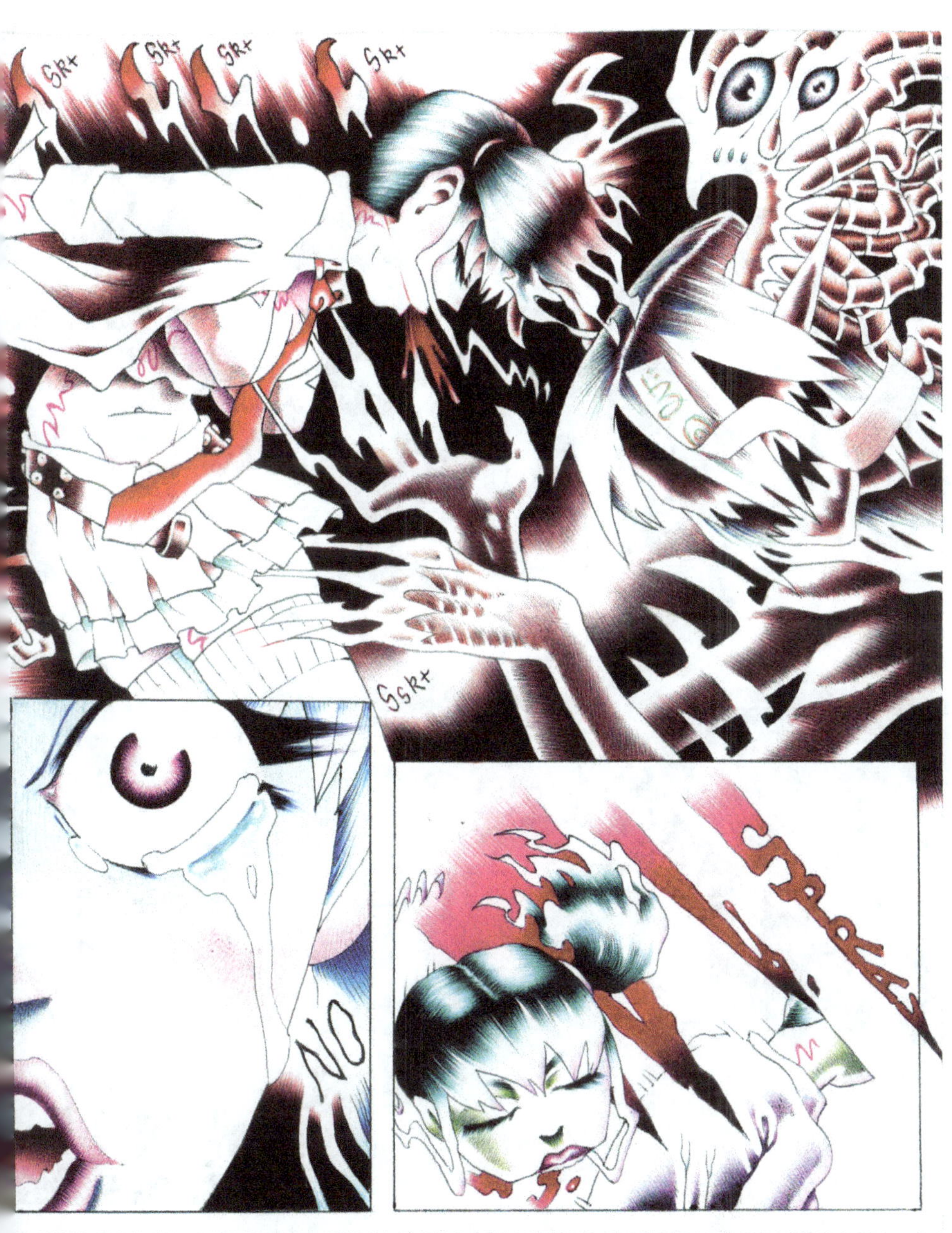

SKt
SKt
SKt
SKt
SSKt
NO

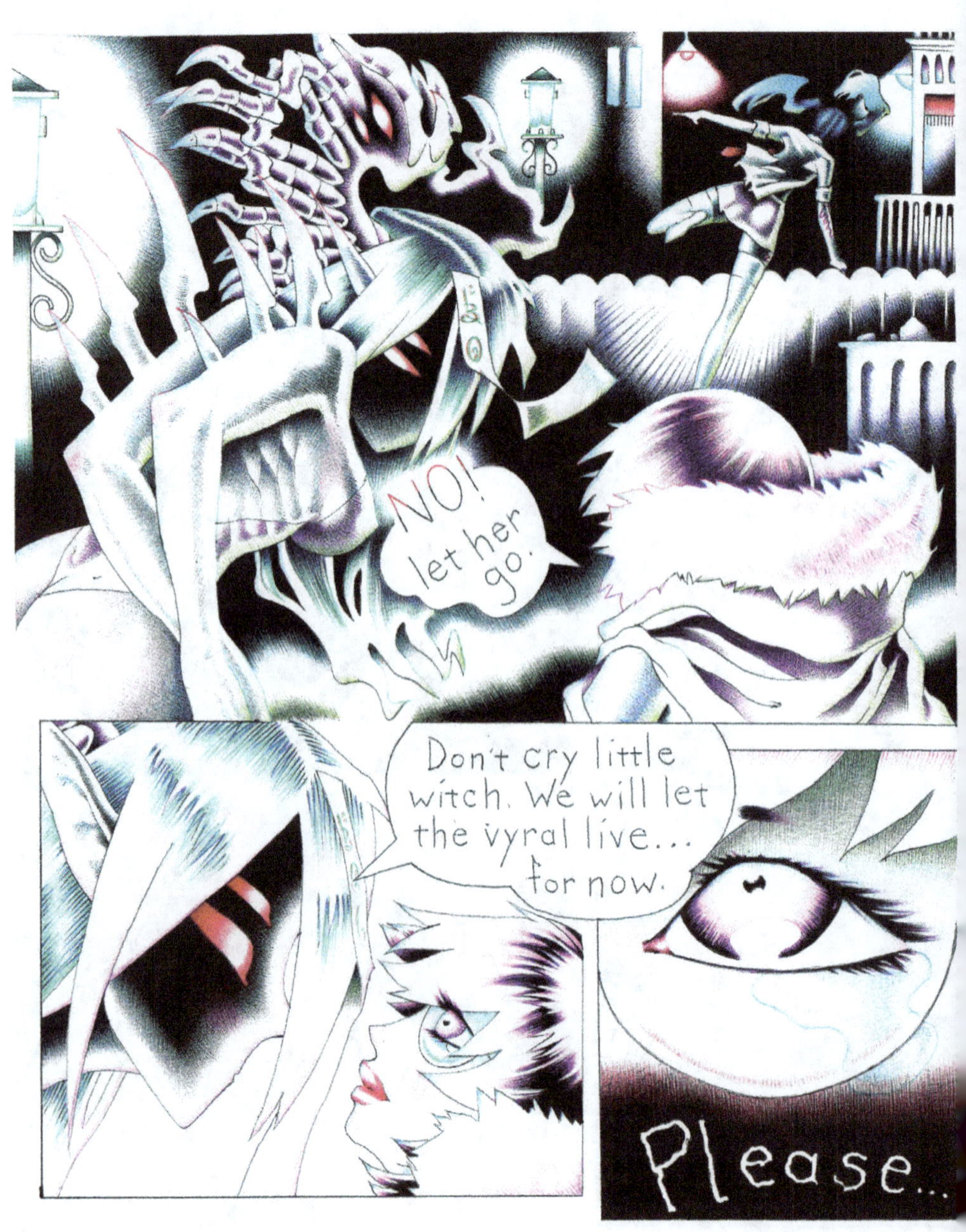

NO! let her go.
Don't cry little witch. We will let the vyral live... for now.
Please...

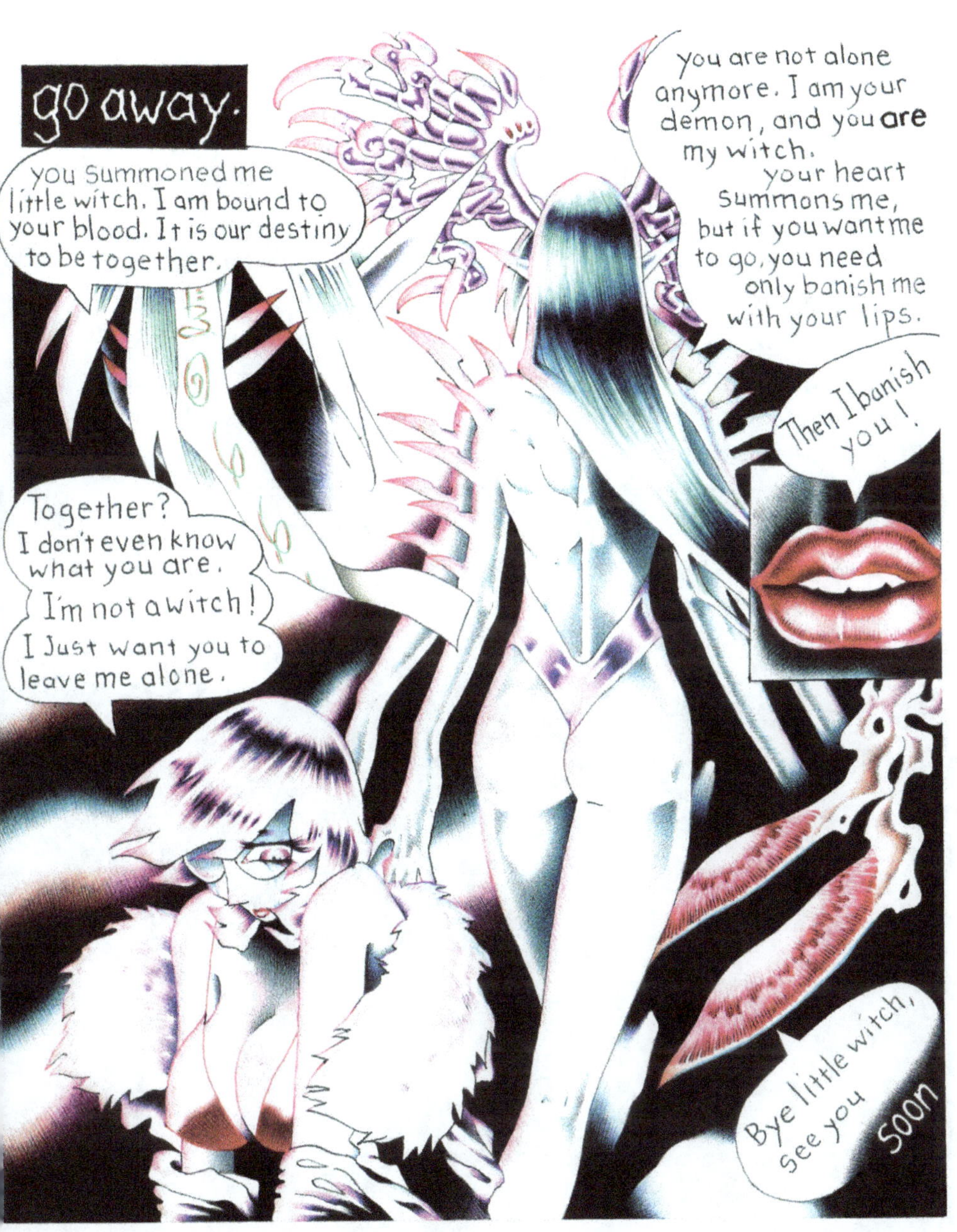
go away.
you Summoned me little witch. I am bound to your blood. It is our destiny to be together.
Together? I don't even know what you are. I'm not a witch! I Just want you to leave me alone.
you are not alone anymore. I am your demon, and you are my witch. your heart Summons me, but if you want me to go, you need only banish me with your lips.
Then I banish you!
Bye little witch, see you soon

"The Journey Through Avalon"

When the rays of the sun become the glow of the moon the fields of Avalon are ripe. The winds blow and the rains become knowledge that fall upon the saint and sinner alike and the serpent arrives with the fruits of wisdom. Will you partake and live as the colors of the rainbow and the horn of the unicorn? In knowing the unknown the unknown becomes the known and we become the clouds that pour out the rain on the three fold planets of Jinkum, Resof and Duwayne. Poured like the lava from a volcanic salamander who leaves tracks of energy as he journeys to the fields of Avalon for his own dose of the unicorn's horn, which causes him to transform into a unimander-sal-acorn. He becomes the unknown knowledge that the serpent brought in the drops of transformation. We will all wear the wings of the three eyed tulip faery and the scales of the cycloptic onyx dragon and on these wings we will return to Avalon where we are once again rebirthed into ourselves.

- Jelly Bean AKA N.E.S.A.

Cats, Bats, & Rug Rats
by Summer Breeze

I was friends with a group of death row inmates at Potosi in Mineral Point, Mo., who were Wiccans. They would tell people they could turn them into mice, rats, rocks, cats and other things. People were afraid of them. I myself was not, I would talk to them and they would tell me that Wicca was not about evil, but building a community of practitioners that did good things. Others used it to prey on the weak, making them believe they could cast love spells on them, pulling out pieces of people hair and making lockets, putting human waste in meals and serving them to unsuspecting diners. One thing I noticed is that true Wicca believers are great people, they dress as much as possible in a way that fit there needs, they listen to certain music and they stick together and flow naturally like river water down stream. I really do wish they could turn some of these dudes into cats & bats & rug rats, that would be awesome, LOL.

✳ Book Of Shadows ✳

Hekas! Hekas!

Este Be Beboi - (x3)
— Spiritual Worning —

Waxing, Waxing
growing, growing
?
_______ power is
Flowing Flowing (x9)

spirit

Air   firer

earth   water

* God's & Goddesses *

1. Ra (m) — Isis (F)   Egypt
2. Pan (m) — Hekate (f) Greece
3. Apollo (m) — Daina (F) Rome
4. Herne (m) — Brigid (F) Europe
5. Ishtar (m) — ? (f) middle east
6. Dagda (F) — ? (f) Ireland

Song of Energy

" Holy Well, Sacred Flame,
Welcome, Welcome,
Remain, Remain. (x9)

Protective Chant

Oh Greacious Lady
day & Night,
proteete us by your
Might, for Thrice around
this Circles Blocked
and bound,
all evil stick in the
ground

Elements.

◇ Airt = Swords = New beginning
♣ Firet = Wands = Dicision
♡ Water = Cups = Fertile/Joy
♠ Earth = Pentacles = Succoess

✳ Rune ✳

ᚠ = F — Fehu   **ᚢ = U** — URUZ   **ᚦ = Th** — Thurisaz

ᚨ = a — Ansuz   **ᚱ = r** — Raido   **ᚲ = K** — Kennaz

ᚹ = w/v — wunjo   **ᚺ = h** — Hagalaz   **ᚾ = n** — nauthiz

ᛁ = i — Isa   **ᛃ = j** — Jera   **ᛉ = z** — Elhaz

ᛇ = ei — Eihwas   **ᛈ = P** — Perthro   **ᛋ = S** — Sowilo

ᛏ = T — Tiwas   **ᛒ = b** — Barkana   **ᛖ = e** — Ehwaz

ᛗ = M — mannaz   **ᛚ = l** — Laguz   **◇ = ing** — Inguz

ᛞ = d — Dagaz   **ᛟ = o** — Othala

The SABBATs

My belief that the Moon being a physical Manifestation of the Power and glory of the Goddess, the sabbat Rites are celebrated at midnight on the night before the day of the festival

I follow eight Great Sabbat and there are thirteen New Moon and thirteen full Moon Esbats in a year.

Our year begains with Yule.

As it is understood Yule starts on December 21, The Winter Solstice. I celebrate the return or rebirt of the Sun.

*Candlemas; February 2; Is Call the Fire festival. This is the Feast of the Waxing Light

*The Spring Rite; March 21 Known as Spring Equinox

* Rudemas; Starts on May 1 A festival of fertility Sabbat

* Baltane - June 21, A midsummer festival (Summer Solstice)

* Lammas; August 1, A Rite for increase

* Autumn Equinox Rite; it's September 21, time of thanks-giving

* Hallowmas; October 31, reunion of Souls

The Twelve Houses

♈, FiRe   1st   Aries, Physicl Body
♌, Red   5th   Leo, The Soul
♐, South, 9th, Sagittarius, the Mind

♉, Earth, 2nb, Taurus, Passion
♍, Green, 6th, Virgo, work/Career
♑, North, 10th Capricorn recognition

♊, Air, 3ed, Gemini, Relationships
♎, Yellow, 7th, Lebra, one to one/Love
♒, East, 11th, Aquarius, friendships

♋, Water, 4th, Cancer, DeAth-Body
♏, Blue, 8th, Scorpio, Soul release
♓, West, 12th, Pisces, Karma

House/month	House/Month	House/Month
Aries 3—4	Leo 8—7	Sagitt. 11—12
Taurus 4-5	Virgo 8—9	Capri. 12-1
Gemini 5-6	Lebra 9—10	Aquar. 1—2
Cancer 6—7	Scorpio 10—11	Pisees 2-3

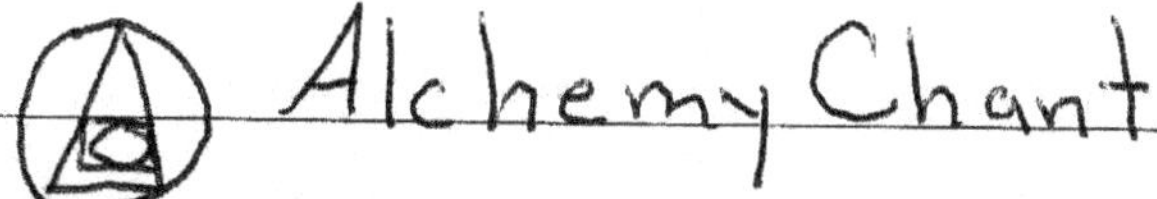 Alchemy Chant

Out of the black and into Red
Out of the Red and into White
Out of the white and into gold
Out of the gold and into world
Where my hand is laid enchantment
is made. As it is above so is
below, so mote it be.

Circle Casting

Black and, White and Gold
Rising Circle taking Hold,

New Moon's Blessing Light
Clear moon Magick stick tight

North is Earth And East Air
Mighty Ones Attend us Here

South is fire and weast is
sea Mighty Ones be with
Me.

I am Priest Levi and
this is just some impart-
tation un to all those waking
this path.
May the Goddess & God
walk with you - Blessed Be

Jeffery Dukes
AKA- Levi
Dukes

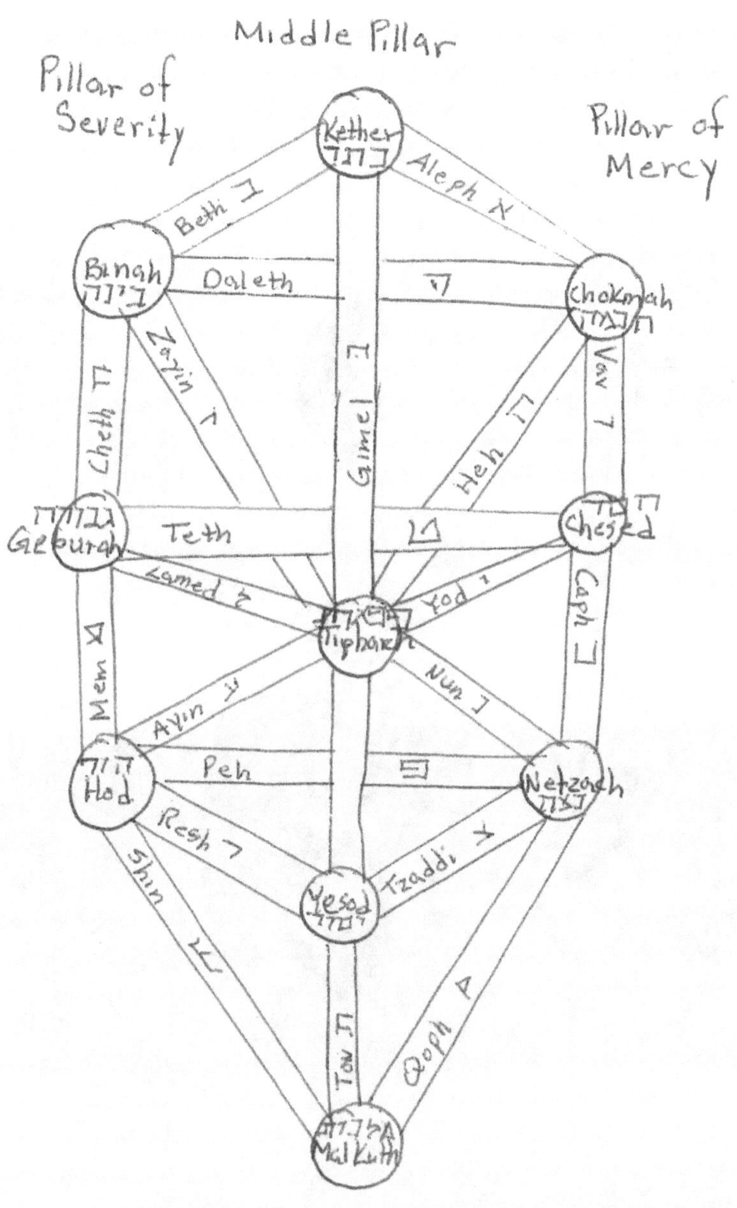

The Tree of Life

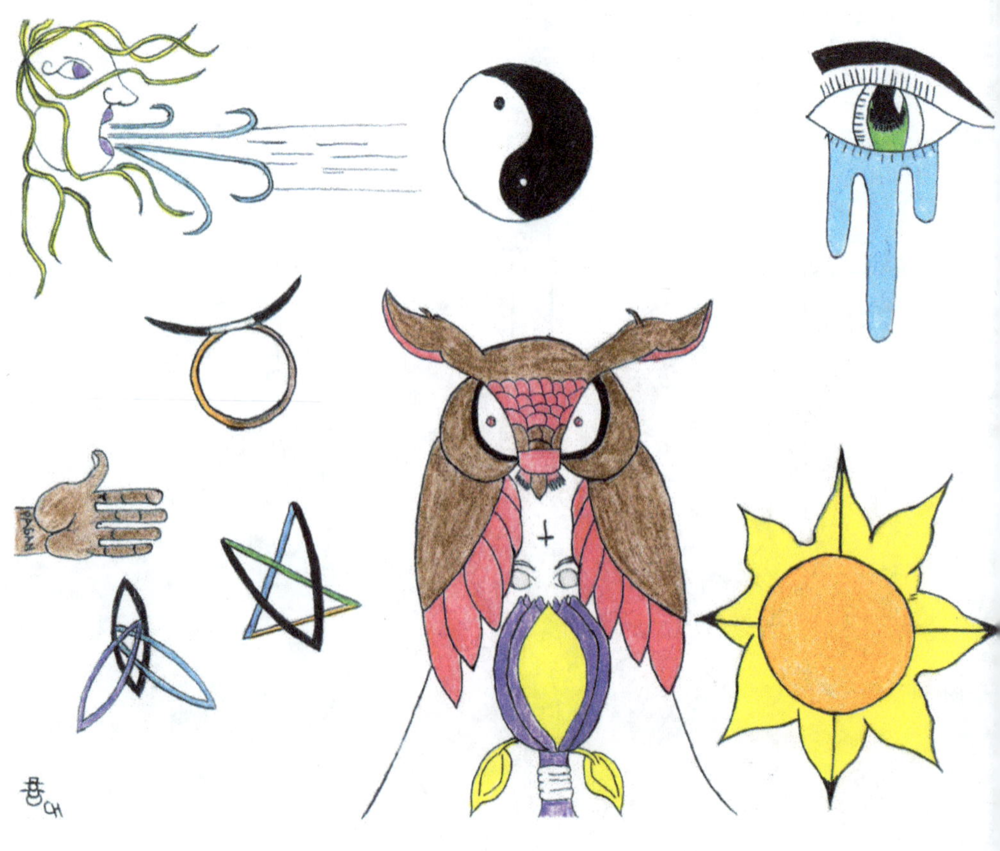

Spiritual Evolution
by John(Winter Born) Cox

I am a professional witch. I not only write and teach the methods of Magick, but perform practical Magick for clients that are seeking to change their lives for the better. Some students and clients are beginners or just regular people in need of a little magical assistance, but many are actual long-term practitioners who just haven't been able to make the Magick work for them. Often, they have dozens of books on the subject and know many spells and rituals, but they just haven't been able to get the results they hoped for. Perhaps they draw spiritual benefit from their path, but they have not been able to make Magick manifest materially in ways that they had expected.

They find themselves having invested a lot of time and effort into an art that they can't seem to make work for them. They may have even built their social lives around Witchcraft and the Occult. Because they haven't been able to do Magick successfully, they may have shifted their focus from the path that originally got them interested, to either Pagan religious observance or psychological self-help. Both are good things. Magick should be used for Spiritual evolution and Mystical insight, but I am here to tell you that Practical Magick does work. Real results are possible; you just need to know how to go about it. Real change in the real world.

Of course there are a lot of books that say that. Magickal books fill the shelves of bookstores all across the world, making all kinds of promises of power and wisdom. How is this book different?

Recently, I took stock of what was out there and noticed that books on Magick generally fell into two categories: Training manuals, or spell books. This book is neither a training manual nor a spell book. It's a Field Guide, from a Witch in the field. There is a lot more to making successful Magick than just Magick itself:

How do you attack a problem from multiple side's using Magick?

How do you blend Magickal and mundane action to achieve success?

How do you know whether what you're doing is working?

How do you fix it if it's not?

What are the best ways to work on behalf of others?

To answer these questions, I will present the usual exercises and spells that you would find in a book of this sort, BUT, more than this, I will present complete strategies for generating successful results. In doing so I will be revealing many tips of the trade that even today are only shared within closed cabals or mentor to student.

It is my hope that this book will aid in rescuing the Art of Magick from those who have ignored, downplayed, or outright denied the existence of Practical Magick in favor or arcane titles, intangible results, and fantasy attainments.

To those who think that spells are only psychological exercises designed to build confidence or release stress or to those who think Witchcraft is only a religion and not a Craft, to those who have come to think that Magick can only affect the mind of the Witch and not the minds of others to those who have tried and failed, and have given up on effecting the fabric of perception and probability - this book intends to prove YOU wrong!

John (Winter Born) Cox
High Priest
Order of the Forbidden Truth
Samhain 2022

Chapter 1: The Gift

Every endeavor in life has a base, a path, and a fruit. Magick is no different, and so we must start by examining our base, the point at which we start. Most books on Magick suggest the base or starting point is the same for everyone, that we all, more or less, are equally talented, and that everyone can accomplish every task with enough effort. Books promising that "Anyone can do it" are as common in the Magick section of bookstores as they are on the self-help and home repairs shelves. Sadly, this isn't necessarily the case.

We are an egalitarian society and like to think that we are all created equal. Although I agree that all life has equal inherent value, that doesn't mean we all are equally gifted at all things. Just as some people are born with innate talent for sports, music, art, or mathematics, some people are born with innate talent for Magick. If you are not particularly gifted in something, you can usually make up for it with hard work and practice, but sadly, just as there are tone deaf people who would love to make music or numerically challenged people who would love to be scientists, there are also people with almost no gift for Magick. Some of you won't like to hear that, but it's true.

In older days, only people who had some gift or calling would have even considered studying Magick. In most cultures, even ones in which Magick is recognized and accepted as real, a career in Magick or spirituality is not something that someone undertakes unless they felt strongly pulled in that direction. Certainly, this strong taboo against Magick in the western world, with penalties ranging from ridicule to execution, has in the past been enough to weed out those who only had a cursory interest. Only those with a burning need would even consider undertaking any type of Occult study.

Today, however, the situation is a bit different. Magick is BIG business, and Witchcraft is VERY popular. Rather than attracting only those who have a gift for the work, the arts attract hundreds of people who have no real calling for, or sometimes even an interest in Practical Magick. They might be interested in Paganism as a religion, or even Magick as a counter cultural statement. Some join a Coven or Order simply because people in their social circle are doing it. These folks may try out a spell or two, but if they don't get immediate results they stop trying because the Magick isn't really what drew them in, in the first place. There is nothing wrong with spiritual development or religion, but if people who aren't interested in or don't even believe in Magick keep calling themselves Witches or Magicians it causes a bit of con-fusion. The world is filled with Witches who cannot perform a simple task of Witchcraft.

Now before you get the idea that only a few lucky souls who are born with a caul, or the seventh son of a seventh son can be a successfully Witch, let me ease your mind by telling you that effort in developing your gift is far more important than your innate gift. Many people have powerful gifts, but no effort into developing them, and thus produce shaky results, if any at all. Conversely, many people, who have only modest gifts but put a lot of time into developing them turn out to be very successful Witches. Besides innate gifts and training, there is another element of the equation for successful Witchcraft: Implementation. You can have amazing gifts at Magick, spend-ing hours every day in meditation, study, and ritual, but still not know how to apply your talents in Practical situations.

Remember the following:

(gift × development) + skillful implementation = success

So how do we know if we have a gift? There are some traditional signs we can look at that appear at birth. Being born on Halloween, having a still born twin or simply not crying as a baby are a few signs that people have pointed to through the centuries as marked of spiritual gifts.

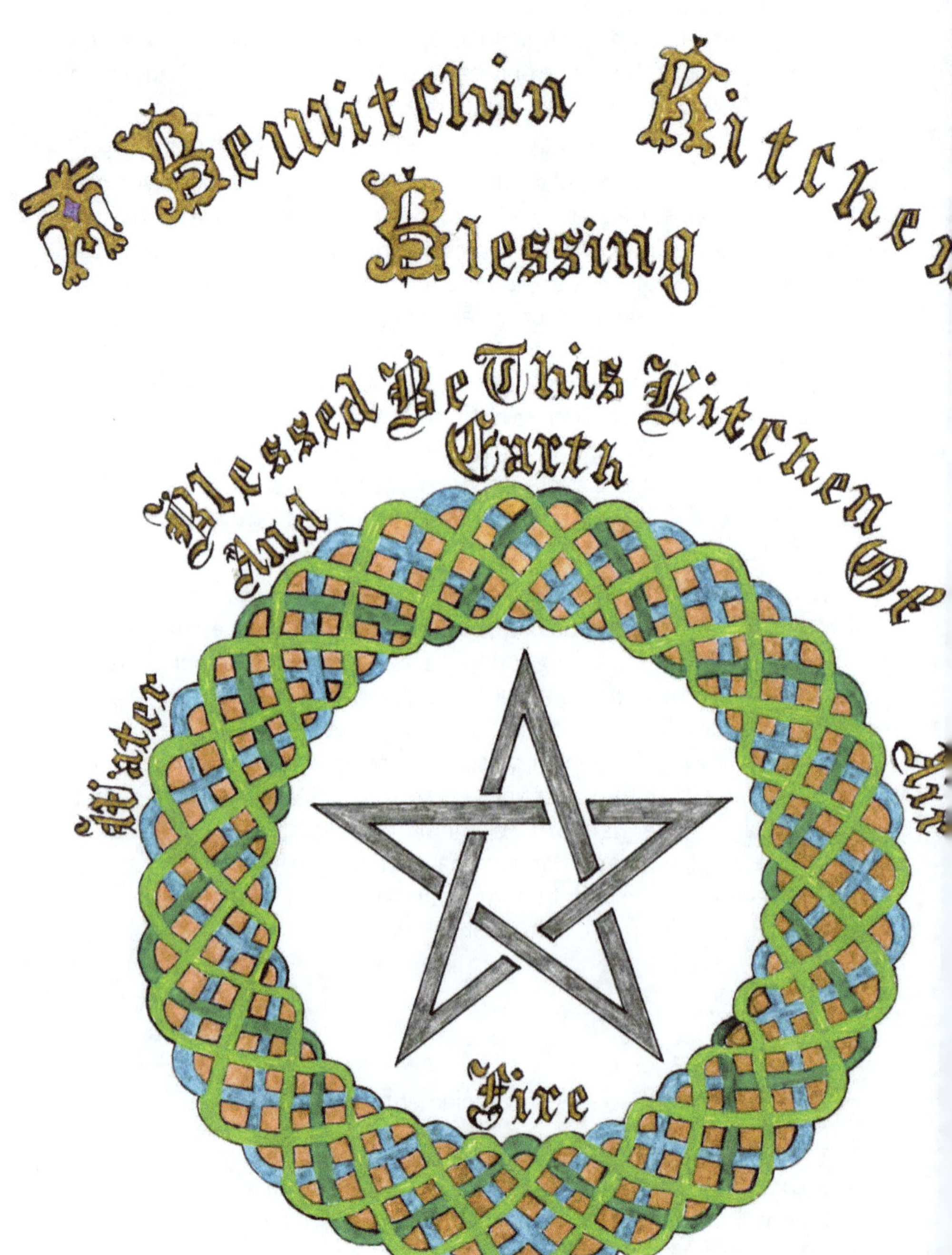
A Bewitchin Kitchen Blessing
Blessed Be This Kitchen Of
Blessed Be This Kitchen Of
Earth
And
Water
Fire
Fire

Author and Artist Biographies

A.D. White

Andrew White (Drew) is a writer from North Carolina, and "Regret" is her very first attempt at creating a comic. Her writings have been published in various places, most notably in Spectral Realms poetry magazine. Drew is a nature lover, a heavy metal fanatic, and a devotee of the Divine Feminine.

Charlie Harbert

I love to read books! From history to fiction and everything in between. I also enjoy writing poems and short stories. This is something I'm very passionate about. I am trying to get some of my work published right now.

Dennis "Abbadunamis" Mintun

My books and articles can be found at: safestreetsarts.info, spotlighton-recovery.com, dhinitiative.org, idahoinsider.net, themarshallproject.org, eveningstreetpress.com and more! All humans are gods in various states of evolution.

Dottie Cornyx

I'm a veteran, Libertarian on a journey of self-discovery and self-acceptance, late in life, while a guest at T.D.C.J.

Eracüs Wolfkrow

Two spirited mixed blood, I was born in Lubbock, TX. I love listening to rock and metal. I love to draw and wish to find true love. If it still exists. Get back at me if you want to talk about my art.

Gary Farlow

A PEN Award winning author and artist whose works are on display with Cornell University, the Justice Arts Coalition, and Open Sky Gallery.

Harlequin

A pansexual trans woman confined in Pennsylvania Department of Corrections. She is an activist, artist and jailhouse lawyer, fighting for the rights of others. She enjoys reading, writing and having fun with friends and family.

janetter xoxo

janette r. is an artist and a guitarist incarcerated in a california prison.

Jeffery Levi Dukes aka Déz

Brothers and Sisters inside, keep fighting the good fight. I need you, the world needs you, your family needs you... I love you all. We have and shall rise.

Jelly Bean AKA N.E.S.A.

I am a practitioner of Wicca and study world religions and just to learn things. I stand out in a crowd because of my tattoos and body mode but also because I identify as a Neon Electric Space Alien!

jennifer amelia rose

An anarchist/antifa prisoner, artist, poetic student, and queer/trans woman writer in California prisons. She's 52 and a co-founder of Fire Ant Collective, an inside organizer for several abolitionist and anti-racist groups including Initiate Justice, TGI Justice Project, Prisoner Correspondence Project, and Incarcerated Workers' Organizing Committee (IWOC) - among others.

Jody Furnare

With all my love and hope: Keep up the Faith, Hold the Love, and with Hope is Solidarity.

John (Winter Born) Cox

A 49 y/o Pansexual man who is Pagan in faith, and deep into Goth, Emo, BDSM and all that goes with it. I am writing a Book on Witchcraft, hopefully to be put into print this year.

John Heden

I'm caring, honest, loyal, open minded, nonjudgmental, and Wiccan. I enjoy painting, music, some sports, cars and writing. I make the most of my time, and refuse to let this place drag me down!

Nicolin Broderway

My biggest accomplishment in life is living. I was handed a pretty rough life. The fact that I am living is proof that you can succeed. I am a survivor and I do not allow the bad to consume me.

Raven Rodriguez

As a girl, I really don't mind helping my family out. I lost my mom, 2 of my sisters who love me to death. I can draw real good, very good with the love of you!

Samantha Dynamite

I'm a Black transwoman, 43 years old and have been an artist (self taught) since age 5. I'm a NERD. I love fantasy, sci-fi, and alien conspiracy theory.

Spark Dalmatian

Has been a dedicated gay furry for 13 years, and has also served as a firefighter/EMT. In his spare time he enjoys music, reading, and trains (both model and real).

Summer Breeze

Also known as Mama Tee, Summer Breeze is an inmate from Missouri who seeks to be the 1st transgender governor :) "Vote for me, I'll set you free!"

Surreal

Currently focusing on reading and studying the Bible to tell people about Jesus Christ. They consider this article as a beautiful memory to hold on to forever.

Tammy Beth Graham

I'm Wiccan, 39 years young, I now consider myself non-binary. I am an artist yet have been focusing solely on my writing for the last few years. I am in the process of writing my own anthology.

Tammy Jean Norman aka Phoenix-Electra

I was initiated in the Celtic-Pagan tradition on October 12th-13th, 1999 by the high priestess Lady Firewind in the Coven of Tears of the Prairie in Ogden, Kansas and I am a devotee and practitioner of the Marrigan ever since.

The Villain Blvme

Diversity in the religious/political/social constructs of norms and morality.

Resources

Aquarian Tabernacle Church

P.O. Box 409, Index, WA 98256

Write to the above address to receive 1 each of published Wiccan and Pagan resources for your prison's library. Include any restrictions your prison has for books.

ASPHODEL PRESS

Candles in the Cave: Northern Tradition Paganism for Prisoners

Explores the prayers and practices of Northern Tradition Paganism, in a version written specifically for prisoners. Each prayer and ritual can be done alone, with only pencil and paper, or not even that. Contemplating Gods in the Walls: Pagan Resources for Incarcerated Transwomen. Prayers and essays of hope for transwomen living behind bars.

Wicca Beyond the Binary: Single-Sex Coven Resources for Incarcerated Wiccans. Wiccan rituals which are not dependent on a male/female binary, plus tips on doing ritual with very few props. The Wiccan Paper Altar: 8.5x11 envelope with printed pieces which can be cut out, set up, and folded flat again. Free by request. Please enclose information about book-shipping policies. Not responsible for books confiscated by mail rooms. Also available to order online- discount only applies if sent directly to a prison. Above books can be sent for no cost to prison chaplains to include in prison library. *Have your chaplain contact us.*

BBI Media

P.O. Box 687, Forest Grove, OR 97116.

www.bbimedia.com
Tel: 503-430-8817
Offers free subscriptions to prison chaplains and prison libraries. Requests must be submitted on official prison letterhead. Its publications include Witches & Pagans and SageWoman (women's facilities only). Witches & Pagans features:
•Interviews with those who create and lead our traditions
•Visits to the sacred places and people who inspire us
•In-depth discussions of our ever-evolving practices
•Practical daily magic
•Ideas for solitary ritual and devotion

•Craft projects
•Pagan poetry and short fiction and reviews

Mother Earth Ministries–ATC

P.O. Box 35906, Tucson, AZ 85740-5906

Mother Earth Ministries' mission is to provide accurate information about Wicca and other Pagan faiths to interested inmates and prison staff in Arizona, and to facilitate Pagan prisoners' study and practice of their religions. In addition to providing brochures and booklets to individual prisoners and prison libraries, Mother Earth Ministries sends priestesses and priests into prisons to counsel, teach, and lead rituals. Other clergy work with inmates by mail, answering questions and directing study. We are limited only by the availability of qualified volunteers and the cost of transportation to outlying prisons.

Pagan Educational Network (PEN)

PO Box 24072, Indianapolis, IN 46224

The Pagan Education Network has a list of organizations, correspondence courses, books, and contacts for pen-pals and specific traditions.

Crow Gleann Pagan Services

PO Box 81214 Simpsonville SC 29680

Crow Gleann helps incarcerated Pagans with their spiritual journey through Wiccan Sabbat newsletters, videos, and educational materials.

We began our journey with the SCDC inmates in 2011. Since then, we have expanded our contact list to volunteers and chaplains in over 30 states.

We partner with other Pagan prison ministries with information on Pagan paths such as Druidry and Asatru.

Our goal is to assist inmates to practice their Pagan faith whether in a group or as a solitary practitioner.

Appalachian Pagan Ministry

PO Box 162, Pomeroy, OH 45769

A pan-Pagan ministry devoted to building an active, passionate, and spiritually fulfilled community of people from all backgrounds and faiths. We are devoted to engaging and impacting other pagans here and within the walls, believing it is our responsibility to set an example of service. This is where we come to "walk our talk" and educate by example. It is the desire of this ministry to show that pagans of all beliefs and faiths CAN work together to serve the greater community.

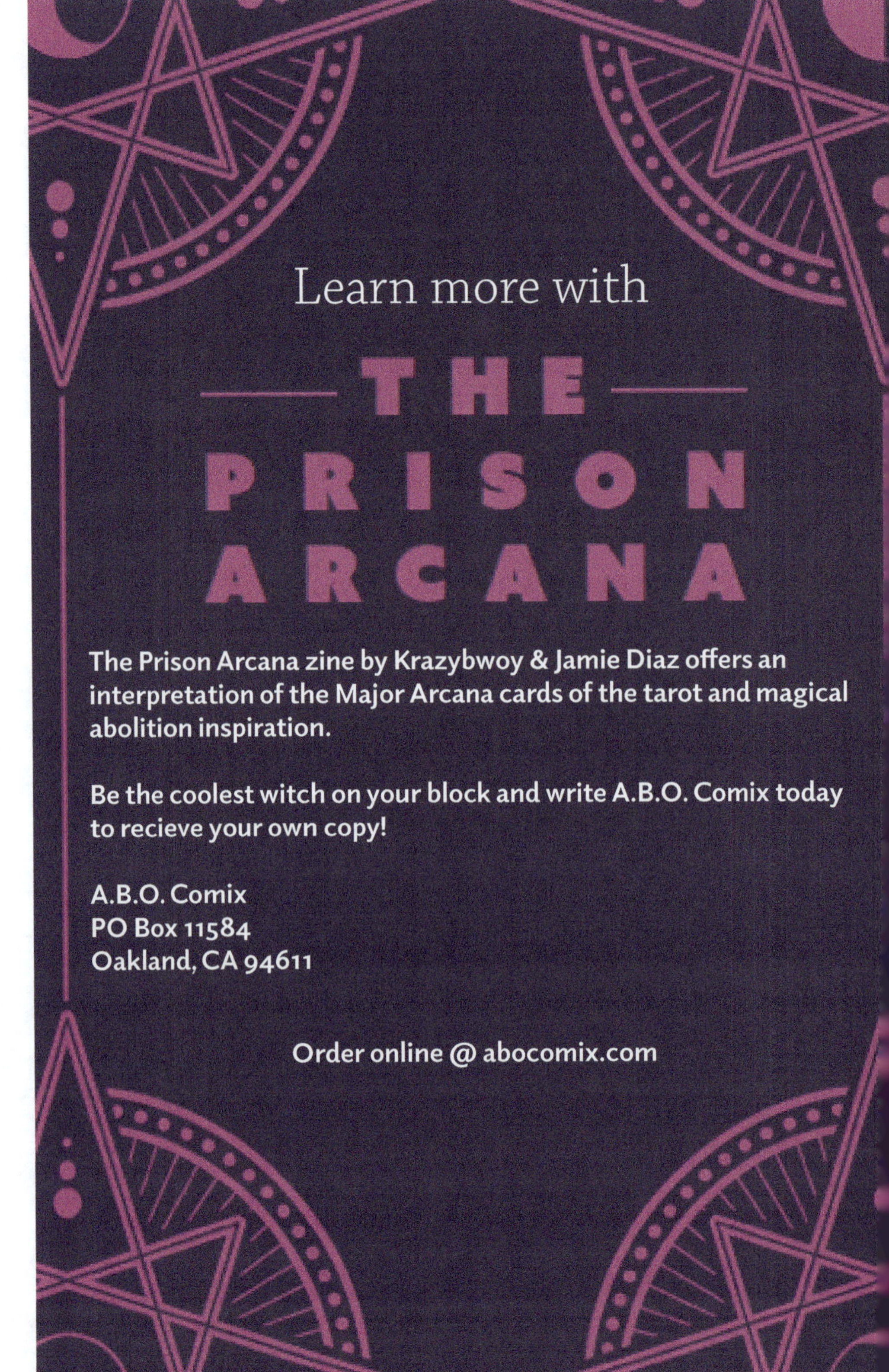

Learn more with

THE

PRISON

ARCANA

The Prison Arcana zine by Krazybwoy & Jamie Diaz offers an interpretation of the Major Arcana cards of the tarot and magical abolition inspiration.

Be the coolest witch on your block and write A.B.O. Comix today to recieve your own copy!

A.B.O. Comix
PO Box 11584
Oakland, CA 94611

Order online @ abocomix.com